THE SPANISH ON THE NORTHWEST COAST

For Glory, God, and Gain

HERITAGE

VICTORIA · VANCOUVER · CALGARY

Heritage House Publishing Company Ltd.
heritagehouse.ca

Library and Archives Canada Cataloguing in Publication
Neering, Rosemary, 1945-, author
The Spanish on the northwest coast : for glory, God and gain / Rosemary Neering.

Includes bibliographical references and index.
Issued in print and electronic formats.
ISBN 978-1-927527-83-2 (pbk.).—ISBN 978-1-927527-84-9 (html).—ISBN 978-1-927527-85-6 (pdf)

1. Northwest Coast of North America—Discovery and exploration—Spanish. 2. Spaniards—Northwest Coast of North America—History—18th century. 3. Explorers—Northwest Coast of North America—History—18th century. 4. Explorers—Spain—History—18th century. 5. Northwest Coast of North America—History—18th century. 6. Indians of North America—Northwest Coast of North America. I. Title.

F851.5.N43 2014   979.5'01   C2013-908569-6   C2013-908570-X

Edited by Karla Decker
Proofread by Liesbeth Leatherbarrow
Cover photo: The Spanish Insult to the British Flag at Nootka Sound (Library of Congress)
Author photo: Rosemary Neering with explorer Juan Francisco de la Bodega y Quadra.
    Photo: Penny Tennenhouse

This book was produced using FSC*-certified, acid-free papers, processed chlorine free, and printed with vegetable-based inks.

Heritage House acknowledges the financial support for its publishing program from the Government of Canada through the Canada Book Fund (CBF), Canada Council for the Arts and the province of British Columbia through the British Columbia Arts Council and the Book Publishing Tax Credit.

18 17 16 15 14 1 2 3 4 5
Printed in Canada

Contents

Prologue

THE WIND HOWLED THROUGH THE *rigging, and high waves slapped over the sides of the tiny schooner* Sonora. *The darkness was almost absolute. Bruno de Hezeta, captain of the sister ship* Santiago, *ordered the crew to fire rockets and then the swivel guns, but little could be heard and less seen on the* Sonora. *Facing into the wind in unknown waters a thousand kilometres from their Mexican base of San Blas,* Sonora *captain Juan Francisco de la Bodega y Quadra tried fruitlessly to keep in touch.*

Hezeta, in overall command, had already argued that both ships should turn tail and head south. But where, questioned the thirty-one-year-old Bodega and his twenty-year-old pilot Francisco Antonio Mourelle de la Rúa, was the adventure, the glory, and the chance of promotion in that? They continued to search for the Santiago, although perhaps not very hard. Alone on the seas, they sailed north into uncharted seas. "I decided to continue the exploration," Bodega wrote in his journal, "in accordance with instructions in spite of realizing that the consequences could be disastrous, so advanced was the season, if we attempted to reach a higher latitude in a ship so small, lacking medicines and surgeons and even water. I pressed on, taking fresh trouble for granted."

Trouble had already plagued the Sonora. The man first named to captain the ship had been seized with madness. The schooner was an unwilling sailor, cramped and miserable. The Sonora's futtocks—midship timbers—were too rotten to hold a nail. The mast had been broken and repaired.

Adverse winds had driven both ships far out to sea; it had taken them almost four months to sail from the coast of Mexico to this point off what would one day be known as Juan de Fuca Strait. Scant weeks earlier, seeking water and wood from the Quinault people on the Olympic Peninsula, Bodega had sent six of his meagre crew of seventeen ashore. Despite earlier friendly relations with the Natives, the Spaniards were killed by some three hundred men, who cut them off from their ship and destroyed its only boat.

Most of their food supplies were aboard the larger Santiago. And already many of the men were fatigued and miserable, slowly succumbing to scurvy, their gums swollen, their limbs aching. But Bodega was resolute. There would be no turning back.

Voyaging for Glory, God, and Gain

A GLANCE AT A MAP of the northwest Pacific coast tells the story: Galiano Island, Malaspina Strait, Quadra Island, San Juan Island, Lopez Island, Guemes Channel, Esperanza Inlet, Florencia Bay, Saturna Island, Juan de Fuca Strait, Camano Island, Cordova Bay, and, far to the north, Puerto de los Dolores, Bucareli Bay, Revillagigedo Island, and Valdez. The names are scattered across the map, a legacy of the voyages of exploration undertaken by Spanish sailors over the course of almost three hundred years.

As early as the sixteenth century, almost two hundred years before Captain James Cook made his celebrated voyage to the Northwest Coast in 1778, adventurers under the Spanish flag were working their way along the coast north from Spanish outposts in Mexico and Baja and Alta California. The earliest of these voyagers brought back amazing tales: some were true, and some were purest invention. But the greatest activity came in a twenty-year time span in the last quarter of the eighteenth century.

By the 1600s, Spain was possessor by claim and conquest of South America from Chile through Ecuador, and much of Central America and Mexico. Their Pacific empire also included the Philippines; the Californias (Baja and Alta); and the American southwest, from Texas north to Colorado and west to the coast. Their possessions in Mexico, Central America, and North America they named New Spain, governed by a viceroy in Mexico City, his orders relayed in long sea voyages from Spain, then overland to the posts on the west coast.

Much remained to be explored and exploited. The motives for journeys up the Northwest Coast were many. Those who sailed into unknown regions might reap glory and the gratitude of their far-off king. Spain, as other countries, sought a northwest passage, a way of moving from the Caribbean and Atlantic to the Pacific Ocean that was simpler and shorter than the long sea journey around Cape Horn or the land journey across the Isthmus of Panama. There were reports of the Straits of Anián, somewhere in mid-northern latitudes, that might connect to the Arctic Ocean and thence to the Atlantic. At the very least, Spain wanted to keep other nations from discovering any such

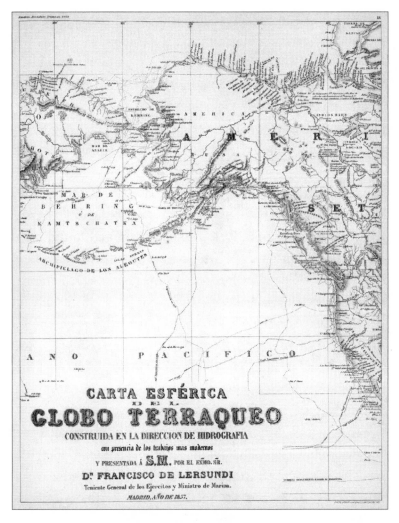

This map, drawn in Madrid in the 1850s, portrays the Northwest Coast as explored by Spaniards over the course of several centuries, with the names conferred by Spain's mariners.

passage, lest sailors and merchants travel through it and intrude on Spanish colonies and their trade.

The Spanish were motivated, too, by the goal of converting Native souls to the Catholic god, as had been done in South America and Mexico. Spain had also garnered great riches in its New World possessions: might there be more gold or other precious items worth seeking farther north?

Glory, God, and gain: each was a driving force that sent Spaniards to the northwest Pacific coast. The conflicts, battles, and alliances of a Europe stirred by frequent war and, eventually, revolution, form the backdrop and foundation for these distant voyages. The Spaniards' efforts were often plagued by failures in communication between the home government in Madrid and the colonial government in Mexico City, and the voyagers who travelled far from both. Other challenges included scurvy, inadequate ships, storms, conflicts, and fallible navigation. And the characters of the men who sailed for Spain—fierce, adventuresome, confrontational, diplomatic—greatly influenced events.

In the end, Spain left the Northwest Coast, and the region itself no longer drew the ships of a dozen countries. Yet, Spain's time in this place was one of great adventure and achievement, and the tales of that time interweave to produce a fine and amazing story.

1

First Approaches

THEY MET IN VENICE, PERHAPS in a bar, perhaps in a private house, the sixty-year-old, greying Greek pilot long in the service of Spain, and the English merchant adventurer, now in his mid-sixties, freed from debtors' prison though not from debts. Their conversation must have been animated, for merchant Michael Lok was ever a believer in and promoter of a northwest passage, and pilot Juan de Fuca claimed he had found just such a thing—or at least the possibility of one.

Juan de Fuca's correct name was probably either Ioánnis Phokás or Apóstolos Valerianos. Adventurer, mariner, and pilot, he was a frequent voyager in the seas surrounding Spain's American empire. In Venice in 1596, he told Lok that some years earlier, he had been aboard a Manila galleon with a great deal of his own funds invested and expecting a fine return. Not far from the California shore, the ship was boarded and ransacked by English freebooter Thomas Cavendish, who was following in the footsteps of renowned English pirate Francis Drake. His hopes and his fortune in tatters, de Fuca took on work as the pilot on Spanish explorations to the north.

His first voyage north was aborted when the crew mutinied against "the Sodomie of their captain." Then, de Fuca told Lok, he sailed north in 1592 with two small Spanish ships, seeking the fabled Straits of Anián, just one hundred years after Columbus reached the eastern outposts of America.

The ships reached somewhere between latitudes 47° and 48° north, he said, where they discovered the entry to the strait, a broad passage marked by a "great Hedland or Iland, with an exceeding high Pinnacle or spired Rocke, like a pillar thereupon." Lok claimed that de Fuca told him this region was rich in silver, gold, and pearls, but this may well have been Lok's invention to spice up the tale, for Lok was eager to see England sponsor new voyages to find a northwest passage.

Did Juan de Fuca, sailing for Spain, actually discover the strait that now bears his name? For many years, historians discredited Lok's claims and even cast doubt on Juan de Fuca's very existence. Spain published no account of the supposed voyage, and de Fuca appears in no official documents. But, in recent decades, the burden of evidence and opinion has moved squarely to de Fuca's side. A galleon such as the one he says was robbed was indeed captured and raided by Francis Drake; a second was waylaid by Cavendish; and both tales mention a pilot who may have been de Fuca. Though Lok's account of the strait is not overly accurate, it does resemble reality, especially given the state of navigation and the difficulties of sailing through the strait in the sixteenth century. If any such voyage had taken place, Spain might well have kept the evidence secret. The voyage of Juan de Fuca was quite probably the first Spanish venture to the Northwest Coast.

What, then, of the supposed voyage of Bartholomew de Fonte in 1640? A London magazine published an account of such a venture in 1708, to little notice. Then a British parliamentarian started the saga toward respectability in 1740, and French geographers accepted it at face value. The account claimed that de Fonte and his fellow Spanish mariners had sailed four ships north from Callao, in Peru, reaching latitude 53° north several months later. There, de Fonte dispatched one of his ships to sail up a "fair river, a gentle stream and deep water" into a lake on whose shores lived a friendly people. The Spaniards happily sustained themselves on an abundance of venison and freshwater fish, wild fowl, and berries. Ever eastward they sailed, until they came to a great bay where a large ship, a trader out of

Boston, was anchored. De Fonte gave the captain his diamond ring and distributed various gifts to the others on the ship. He continued east and then south, taking the apparently short route back home.

Did this voyage ever take place? Whether it was fact or fiction, Spain would spend much time and money in the eighteenth century trying to prove or disprove the story of de Fonte's journey. (For the answer, see chapter 11.)

In another tale, Lorenzo Ferrer Maldonado claimed to have sailed across the top of North America from the Atlantic to the Pacific in 1609. Was there any truth to his story? Though it seems total fiction, the route he describes corresponds to the actual route of the Northwest Passage. Is it possible that he did indeed sail through the Arctic Ocean in a warm year when the passages were ice-free? If he did, then he was one of the first Spaniards to visit the Northwest Coast.

Whatever the truth of these stories, adventurers and explorers in the days of sail faced no easy task in the North Pacific. Great advances had been made in navigation by the sixteenth century with the use of the thirty-two-point magnetic compass and the evolution of dead reckoning—a method of calculating position by measuring the speed of a ship and the time elapsed from a known prior position to determine the present position. But, given winds, tides, and current, such calculations could be only approximate.

Sailing ships were, of course, always governed by the wind. Spanish ships that left Acapulco loaded with gold and other valuables, headed for Manila, had a relatively simple journey west, one that took about four months to complete. But Portuguese warships barred the southern route back to Spain via the Indian Ocean. The Spanish Manila galleons, now loaded with trade goods such as silks and beeswax, had to return instead to Acapulco, travelling against the winds. Their route described a great curve northward to Japan, then out across the Pacific. Once signs of land such as floating debris, seabirds, and sea mammals appeared, they could turn south along the invisible coast to Mexico. The voyage took six months.

They were not pleasant months. Though beautiful to behold, the galleons were ungainly and overweight. The space below decks was cramped, crammed with sailors, supplies, and trade goods. One man who sailed aboard a galleon described the hunger, thirst, cold, the need to be continually on watch for pirates and other hazards, the endless battering of the waves, and "a universale raging itch," as well as what the Spanish called *gorgojos* (weevils), "so swift that they in a short time not only run over cabins, beds, and the very dishes the men eat on, but insensibly fasten on the body." Flies, maggots, and other vermin were common—so many maggots and gorgojos, in fact, recounted the traveller, that "I doubted whether the dinner was fish or flesh." Water was in short supply and fresh food non-existent. Scurvy was a constant menace.

Given the difficulties, should Spain devote time and

endless resources to exploring the Pacific coast of the Americas north of Mexico? Opinion was divided. Some said yes, while others thought that riches and a staging stop for the Manila galleons were more likely to be found on some yet undiscovered island in the mid-Pacific. But, in 1602, the supporters of Northwest exploration were in the ascendant, and three Spanish ships headed north from Acapulco. Though they reached such points as Monterey and Cape Mendocino, their expedition could not continue. The majority of the sailors aboard one ship fell ill with severe scurvy, and the ship was forced to turn back lest almost everyone aboard die of the malady. So debilitated were the crew members that the officers had to do the sailors' work of furling sails and making meals. Forty-eight men died before the ship got back to Acapulco.

Cold and scurvy dogged the other ships as well, killing Captain Martin de Aguilar and some of his men. Somehow, all the ships struggled home to Acapulco, and the surviving officers reported the discoveries made on the expedition. The men said they had found, at about latitude 43° north, a "voluminous river" with a fine harbour at its mouth and such an outward flow that they could make no progress up it. Was this, then, the river that led to a northwest passage? They named the river Rio de Martin Aguilar; the search for it would occupy the Spanish a century and a half later.

The evidence of one other visit is well documented. Early in the nineteenth century, American fur traders who reached the mouth of the Columbia by land heard tales of descendants of a group of Spaniards shipwrecked more than a hundred years before. The traders met a red-haired man and another, older man who seemed to be the grandson and son of these Spaniards. As well, the Clatsop First Nation of the area had long before found the remaining wreckage of a vessel and great quantities of beeswax in the sand. In all probability, this was what remained of one of the Manila galleons. The large bales of beeswax, originating in Cambodia or Thailand, were carried on the galleons to Acapulco and thence to Spain, where millions of candles were needed to light homes and other buildings, and to burn on the altars of thousands of churches.

Whatever the truth of the various legends, Spain undoubtedly sent expeditions to explore the Northwest Coast in the sixteenth and early seventeenth century. But then the story falls silent. It would be difficult, no matter how hard they tried, for Spain to keep secret any discoveries—especially of a northwest passage. If the mariners of other nations came to know of such a passage, they could easily enter the Pacific and challenge Spain's territorial claims, bring terror to its settlements, and capture its ships and goods. Stretched thinly along the Pacific coast, Spain would be unable to resist. Better by far not to know, and definitely, not to publish such knowledge, even if they had it.

Back in the Game

THE HAIDA PADDLERS STROKED THEIR great canoes out from the shore, chanting as they neared the Spanish ship. They sang and danced, and then one man sprinkled feathers on the water, making gestures that the Spanish took as tokens of welcome. The Spanish mimicked welcome in return, and the Haida paddled closer. Juan Pérez, captain of the *Santiago,* was delighted when even more canoes showed up when he returned the next day. And the members of the 1774 expedition, the first to the northwest Pacific coast in more than 170 years, rejoiced at the sight of land.

It had been a hard century and a half. For most of those years, Spain had other things on its mind: the Eighty Years' War (1568–1648), the Thirty Years' War (1618–1648), the

War of the Spanish Succession (1701–1714), as well as wars of Catholic against Protestant, empire against empire, in Europe and abroad. Scarcely a decade passed when Spanish troops were not on the move, garnering fear and respect wherever they entered battle.

In those years of conflict, England, Ireland, Spain, the Netherlands, the great expanse of the Holy Roman Empire, Sweden, Denmark, Portugal, and a handful of principalities engaged in a tug of war across the European continent and the surrounding seas, seeking in some cases supremacy, in others, independence. The tangle of wars and battles that had engaged the armies of eight countries and quasi-countries finally came to an end in 1678.

Then, when Charles II of Spain died in 1700, two candidates were proposed to succeed him, one backed by the French, a second by the Austrian Empire. The resulting War of the Spanish Succession, with almost all of Europe involved through intertwining alliances, raged for thirteen years until 1714, when the French candidate, Philip V, was finally installed.

Though the European wars weakened Spain, the country still ruled a vast region in the New World, depending on the silver and gold from Peru and Mexico to finance its trade across the Pacific, and continuing to subjugate the peoples of South America and Mexico. War broke out once more, between Britain and Spain, though this conflict endured just two years. Spain nonetheless had to battle Britain for supremacy in Florida as late as 1740.

The events of these turbulent years made Spain profoundly uneasy. It was clear that the British were ever attempting to expand their sphere of influence, seeking out new colonies and mounting a determined search for a northwest passage. English and Dutch privateers still roamed the Pacific seeking prey, and something must be done to protect the Manila galleons and establish a better base for rest and repair. If Spain wanted to keep alive its claim to the Pacific coast of North America, it could no longer sit idle in its Mexican and South American colonies and expect no incursions into the northern territory. It would have to perform more acts of possession and establish more settlements within that territory.

Britain was not the only nation threatening Spanish interests. By the late seventeenth century, Russia, now officially renamed the Russian Empire, had conquered and pacified the vast extent of Siberia and had established settlements on its Pacific coast. Spain had employed its foreign adventurer, Juan de Fuca; now Russia was delighted to give work to the Danish explorer Vitus Bering. Bering set out from Siberia in 1728 and discovered Bering Strait. Thirteen years later he left Petropavlask, on the Kamchatka Peninsula, and headed north and east with two ships. He sighted land on the east side of Bering Strait, then voyaged south to latitude 55°21′ north, in sight of land. His companion ship, captained by Aleksei Chirikov, dipped south to 47°, but out of sight of land.

Bering and many of his crew died of exposure and scurvy after his ship ran aground and they were forced to winter on a rocky northern island. The survivors struggled back home to Russia on a handmade craft, taking with them the pelts of sea otters they had acquired from the Native Aleuts. The lustrous sea otter furs were an immediate hit and earned the sailors a fortune. Soon, Chinese demand for the pelts would bring Russian, American, and English traders to bays, coves, and islands from Bering Strait south to San Francisco, and the trade would dominate Northwest Coast history for more than sixty years.

Spain was late to hear of the Russian explorations. Because of yet another spat over royal succession, Spain sent no ambassador to St. Petersburg for the twenty years that followed Bering's last expedition. When relations finally resumed, the new Spanish ambassador sent home the story of that expedition and others, an account so detailed that it must have been obtained by espionage. The ambassador, though, was not unduly concerned by the Russian moves. Not so the next ambassador—when the Vizconde de Herreria arrived in Russia, he warned that forays the Russians were now planning posed a definite danger to Spanish interests north of Mexico.

Herreria's report coincided with the appointment of a new *visitador* (financial overseer) to Mexico. José de Galvéz quickly took note of Russian activities and saw the need to protect Spain's interests. He feared that the Russians would soon threaten as far south as Monterey Bay. He directed, therefore, that new missions like those in Baja California should be established in Alta California and that expeditions should be sent north toward Bering Strait to officially hoist Spain's flag wherever ships might land Spaniards ashore. They should map the coast, and soldiers, priests, and settlers should move north, defending the region, converting the Native peoples, and exploiting whatever wealth they might find.

To make this happen, Spain needed to establish a better supply base and port than Acapulco, which lay too far south to sustain northern expansion. To almost everyone's later dismay, the Spaniards chose San Blas, a protected harbour north of today's Puerto Vallarta. The site had good sources of fresh water and timber for building ships but, as later generations would discover, it was hot, marshy, and mosquito-ridden, home to malaria and other tropical diseases. Whenever they could, the naval officers who were based here fled inland to the much more pleasant city of Tepic, but those who built the ships, supplied them, and supervised the workers were forced to remain in the unhealthy and unpleasant climate. The drawbacks of San Blas would also determine the timing of all further voyages north, for conditions at the port dictated that expeditions originating here must leave between November and May, when the place was somewhat tolerable.

Their base established, the Spanish set out to found

missions in Alta California. By 1774, five such existed, from San Diego to Monterey. Though Galvéz and the viceroy of New Spain had much more ambitious plans for the Northwest, they had to deal with other problems in the region before they could embark on those plans. Rebellious Natives in the province of Sonora took up arms against the Spanish, and Spain had to send soldiers to put down the revolt. Galvéz set up new financial and accounting systems and greatly raised government revenues. When King Charles III expelled the Jesuits from their positions of power and as missionaries, Galvéz had to deal with riots and rebellion, for the Jesuits were popular in New Spain. To fill their roles, he brought in Franciscans and Dominicans to work in Baja and in the new Alta California missions.

It was all too much for him. He fell physically, and then mentally, ill. Treated by bleeding and confinement, as was common in that era, he imagined he was the King of Prussia and Sweden, eventually comparing himself to the Eternal Father himself. Taken back to the Mexican interior from the coast, he finally recovered, not the last to be driven mad by the vicissitudes of San Blas.

His plans, however, proceeded. The Russians, the Spanish court was informed, were moving ever farther south, establishing fur-trading posts as they went, and more must be done to push them back. According to rumour, the British were ready to sail through a yet undiscovered northwest passage. If the Russians or British founded settlements in territory Spain claimed, the threat to her colonies in Mexico and South America would be extreme, and it would be difficult to protect the very valuable commerce that existed in those colonies. The new viceroy of New Spain, Antonio Maria de Bucareli y Ursúa, was ordered to strengthen the new missions in Alta California and send exploring expeditions farther north.

Chosen to lead an expedition that would leave San Blas in 1774 was Juan José Pérez Hernández. Pérez was just a pilot in the navy, a junior in rank who would not normally lead such a voyage. But there was no one more senior at San Blas, and Pérez was honoured to be chosen and eager to be under way. He would captain the *Santiago*, a frigate and the largest ship yet built at San Blas, though just twenty-five metres long and eight broad.

The list of supplies for the ship, some of which were destined for the California missions, provides a capsule description of life aboard ship and in the missions: jerked beef, dried fish, hardtack, lard, beans, rice, lentils, cheese, salt, spices, and such necessary luxuries as cinnamon, powdered chocolate, brandy, and wine. That they took aboard lemon syrup and a concoction made from cactus plants suggests they knew how to deal with scurvy, yet that condition would bedevil every voyage into the north. Crowded on deck were a dozen bulls, two dozen sheep, fifteen goats, and seventy-nine chickens, most of them destined for the missions. The ship also carried a good supply of armament, with six cannons, thirty-six muskets with bayonets, thirty-six machetes, and a good deal of ammunition. Somehow, there was still room for the crew on the cramped vessel: eighty-four men, including fourteen gunners, two cooks, and carpenters and caulkers for the inevitable times when the ship must be careened and repaired.

Fearing that if the Russians or British learned of the voyage, they would act quickly to arrive on the coast first, the crew had made all preparations in secret. Pérez was given instructions, but he was not to open them until he left Monterey, for there were, presumably, spies everywhere. He sailed from San Blas in late January of 1774 and arrived at San Diego, where he remained, for reasons unclear, for twenty-five days. Leaving San Diego, he arrived at Monterey, where he stayed for another twenty-six days, finally departing on May 8. Now he could open his instructions and find out exactly what he had been commanded to do.

The letter instructed him to sail north as far as he could. If he reached latitude 60° north, he could turn back south, staying in sight of the coast as much as possible. He should go ashore wherever possible and take formal possession of the land. At the same time, he should acquire fresh water and the wood needed to fuel the cooking stoves on the ship. He was not to start any settlements but was to make note of any places where a settlement might be founded. In such places, he should erect a large cross where it might be seen from the sea and build a cairn of stones in which he should place a glass bottle containing a formal document of possession.

Should he find sites where foreign nationals were living, he was to avoid contact but observe as much as he could of who they were and what they were doing, then sail north of any such settlements and take possession for Spain of those lands. He must try to avoid contact with any other ship he intercepted, but, if contact were unavoidable, he should not say what he was doing, explaining instead that he was taking supplies to Alta California and had, unfortunately, been blown far off course.

If he found Native people ashore, he should give them presents and find out as much as he could about who they were and how they lived, including what metals, crops, plants, and domestic animals they had. He should determine as best he could if they had seen other ships or other foreigners, and ask what these people were doing, where they came from, where they were going, and if they were coming back. He should treat any Natives well, doing nothing by force and everything in friendship, constraining his crew to do the same.

And all of this, if accomplished, would be well rewarded by His Majesty, the king.

The prevailing winds in the North Pacific dictated that any sailing ship that wanted to explore the far Northwest Coast should first sail northwest, then north to intersect the coast before sailing south again. Pérez and the *Santiago* proceeded as recommended. The fog, darkness, and adverse winds were constant threats; the crew could only pray they did not founder on shoals or shore. Two and a half months out of Monterey, they sighted land at the south end of the Alaska Panhandle, the first proven Spanish sighting on the Northwest Coast. Soon after, three great canoes emerged from the Queen Charlotte Islands (now Haida Gwaii), paddled by some fifty chanting Haida men. They made gestures of welcome, but would approach no closer than a musket's range away. When Pérez made welcoming gestures in return, they drew alongside and were soon happily trading with the crew.

They offered otter, bear, and seal pelts, woven blankets, and dried fish. In return, they accepted knives, beads, metal, and clothing. The *Santiago* pulled away for the night; when it returned the next day, more canoes arrived, each carrying some twenty men and women. They were most eager for any metal that had cutting edges, and for abalone shells, fine additions to the less beautiful local shells they used to adorn their blankets and capes.

Though there were the inevitable difficulties in communication between men who did not know each other's languages, the Spaniards noted all that they could see, hear, or deduce, and made the first journal entries about the Northwest Coast First Nations. Two of the Haida came aboard the *Santiago*; two sailors disembarked into a canoe. All went well, except that Pérez was at the mercy of the winds and tides: he could not find a place to anchor. Nonetheless, he stayed for four days. Because he was somewhat distrustful of what might happen if he went ashore, he did not send a landing party. Instead, he said goodbye and headed south once more.

Often now, the fog was too heavy or he was forced to sail too far offshore to see the land. Pérez was a careful voyager—not for him were the reckless feats of later explorers. He never wanted to risk losing his ship and thus quite probably the lives of the crew and his own life. He did sight the coast of Vancouver Island on his route south, but, not surprisingly, did not recognize it was an island. On August 8, he was finally able to drop anchor off Nootka Sound, the protected opening a third of the way down the island's west coast, which he named Surgidero de San Lorenzo. It was the first confirmed sighting by Europeans of the sound that was to play such a large part in subsequent events. He tried to enter the sound in the ship's launch and perhaps go ashore, but the *Santiago* swung in the wind and he had to bring the launch back on board and cut the ship's anchor free.

Several canoes of Nuu-chah-nulth gathered to trade. Some came aboard the *Santiago*, and one or two slipped a couple of silver spoons into their clothing. It was a petty and little mourned loss for the Spaniards, but the spoons would prove significant. When Captain James Cook arrived at Nootka three years later, he saw the spoons in the possession of the Nuu-chah-nulth, and realized that the Spaniards had indeed been the first Europeans at Nootka. But no

Spaniard had gone ashore, and much would be made of this failure when nations fought over possession of the region.

Pérez left Nootka and sailed on south, bypassing Juan de Fuca Strait. Later, Pérez's second-in-command, Estéban José Martinez, claimed he had seen the entrance to the presumed strait, but that Pérez had refused to go closer for fear of rocks or shoals. Martinez would soon return to the region, becoming a key figure in Nootka Sound history. The captain and crew did sight Mount Olympus and columns of smoke rising from First Nations' villages.

His crew severely beset by scurvy, Pérez saw no reason to tarry. The *Santiago* returned to San Blas, and Pérez sent news of the journey to the viceroy. Bucareli was not pleased with the results. Much time, energy, and money had been spent to send the expedition north, and now they had returned without having performed any acts of possession or having landed anywhere on the coast, and having charted very little of the coastline. Yes, he wrote to Madrid, the weather had been bad and the fears many, but surely that was to be expected on such a voyage. They should have done more; they should have done better. The only good news was that the men had found no evidence of British or Russian settlement.

But seeing none did not mean that none existed. Spain must secure possession and protect itself. Further expeditions would have to go north as soon as possible.

3

Trouble to Be Expected

JUAN FRANCISCO DE LA BODEGA Y QUADRA was deeply disappointed. Together with five other junior officers in the Spanish navy, he had set out from Spain with high hopes. They had sailed the Atlantic to Vera Cruz, crossed the land to Mexico City, spent six weeks in the Mexican capital, and finally arrived in the Pacific port of San Blas early in 1775 after six months of travel. The young men had been sent to bolster the Spanish presence on the Pacific coast of Mexico, to strengthen control of Alta California, and to venture northward along the coast. Bodega was greatly anticipating being part of any expedition thrusting into the northern sea.

He was older than most of his companions and in the navy since he was eighteen. He had acquitted himself well in his tour of duty in the Caribbean. He held the same rank of lieutenant as the others. But he was ordered to remain in Tepic, not to sail on the voyage that would soon set out for the Northwest Coast. Bruno de Hezeta, at twenty-four, seven years younger than Bodega, was named captain of the frigate *Santiago* and commander of the entire expedition. Juan Pérez would be his second-in-command, aboard the *Santiago*. Another of the six travellers, Juan de Ayala, would captain the *Sonora*, a schooner that would accompany the *Santiago*. Passed over partly because the others had attained their ranks before he had, and probably partly because he had been born in South America rather than in Spain, Bodega would have to wait ashore at least until the following year.

This, Bodega was not prepared to do. Swallowing his pride and refusing to give in to his disappointment, he volunteered to serve as second-in-command of the *Sonora*. Francisco Antonio Mourelle de la Rúa also chose to go on the *Sonora*. A fine cartographer and well schooled in natural history and ethnology, he would become a good friend and companion to Bodega and write journals that provided the best description of the voyage.

Their offers accepted, the officers began preparations for the journey north. As a large part of their mission, they would be surveying and charting their route. They had brought with them from Spain seven cases of sextants, azimuth compasses, astronomical clocks, telescopes, and other navigational and surveying instruments to make use of the courses in navigation, chart making, and other arts they had taken back in Spain. All this was loaded aboard the ships. They also took aboard provisions sufficient for a year and enough trade goods to endear themselves to any Native people whom they met.

Hezeta was commanded to sail in company with the supply ship *San Carlos* to California, then to continue northward to reach latitude 65° north. Turning south, he was to explore and chart the coast, take possession of the land where possible, treat well any First Nations people he met, and trade with them.

The three ships left San Blas on March 16, 1775. As was frequently the case in such expeditions, drama stalked the voyage, though initially from an unusual source. Three days from port the captain of the *San Carlos*, Miguel Manrique, another of the six officers from Spain, lost his reason, shooting at random and wounding a crew member. Officers aboard the *Santiago*, where he was taken, tried bloodletting and what medicines they had, but, as in the case of Galvéz, the treatment only made matters worse. Manrique shouted and wept and was clearly not fit for service. He was sent back to San Blas in the launch. Ayala was named captain of the *San Carlos*, and Bodega became captain of the *Sonora*.

Though he was content with his position, he was less content with the ship. "A deck and tiny cabin," wrote Mourelle, "were all it had for security or living quarters, with no chests or other baggage than a bunk and what could be contained in a box underneath; the height and width of the space for the crew was [such] that they had to remain in a sitting position; the meagre deck would not allow the convenience of a walk; and in this inactive manner we lived for ten months."

Perhaps more important, the schooner, built near San Blas, was not a good sailor. Small and slow, it could not keep up with the *Santiago* and even had to be towed by the larger ship at one point. Every time the crew—most of them inexperienced sailors who had been ranch hands ashore and had never before been to sea—attempted a task, they were soaked by the waves that broke over the deck. There was little room for supplies, a good part of which had to be carried aboard the *Santiago*.

The *San Carlos* stayed in California, delivering supplies, and the two other ships sailed north. As was the custom in the Spanish navy, Hezeta convened a meeting—a *junta*—to decide whether to put in at Monterey, with the delay that this stop would occasion. Both Bodega and Mourelle were adamant that they should continue north without stopping; they could, they considered, effect repairs en route. Wrote Mourelle, "As to what is said of the condition of the schooner with all its futtocks split and totally useless, unable to hold a nail, and that this damage can have disastrous results because of the strong and continuous winds, none of this appears to me to be a sufficient reason to delay the expedition." Hezeta somewhat reluctantly agreed.

Sailing for the most part distant from the shore, they sighted the northern California coast on June 7 at Trinidad Bay, where they were greeted by canoes of Natives who came out to meet and trade with them. Forty Spaniards went ashore to take possession, erect a cross, obtain wood and water, and make new spars for the ships. "The crew marched in two bodies," wrote Mourelle, "who adored the holy cross upon disembarking, and when at the top of the mountain formed a square, the center of which became a chapel. Here the holy cross was again raised, the mass celebrated, with a sermon, and possession taken. We also fired both our musquetry and cannon which naturally made the Indians suppose we were irresistible." This or a similar formal possession ceremony, venerating God and the king, would be repeated each time Spaniards went ashore in a new location for the next two decades.

Sailing north again, they sighted Vancouver Island on June 18, but wind and waves drove them south again, and the topmast snapped on the *Sonora*. With the ship on its beam ends and threatening to capsize, they managed to turn into the wind and make repairs. It was with relief that they again sighted land, on the Olympic Peninsula coast, and carefully came toward the shore.

With the *Santiago* standing offshore, the *Sonora* threaded through sandbanks and shoals so men from both ships could land. Many Quinault came to meet them, bringing salmon and other seafood to trade. Twenty of the

Spaniards held a possession ceremony the following day, and then six men and the boatswain from the *Sonora* went back ashore in their small boat to take on fresh water, cut firewood, and find a spar to replace the topmast. No sooner had they neared shore than the Quinault rushed at them, killing most. Watching horrified from the ship through his spyglass, Bodega could do nothing. Two of the Spaniards were able to reach the water, but their wounds and the chill of the ocean gave them no chance of making it back to the ship. Their only boat in enemy hands, the Spaniards pushed a barrel overboard and tried to reach the survivors, but to no avail. Then nine canoes with thirty men on each pulled hard for the ship, defended only by Bodega, Mourelle, five men, a boy, and four more crew members, who were ill. As soon as the Quinault came within range, the Spanish fired the swivel gun and their muskets, killing some of the attackers. With one man sounding for shoals and another making cartridges, the helmsman got under way in the faint wind and the schooner eased its way back out to deeper water and the company of the *Santiago*.

Bodega wanted to return with thirty armed men to seek out and punish this "execrable evil," but a majority in the *junta* demurred: their position was too precarious, and they must opt for keeping their ships safe. Now they had to decide if the *Sonora* should, with its depleted crew and poor state of repairs, go on or turn back. Hezeta was concerned. He expressed his doubts about the ability of the smaller ship to keep up, and his concerns about the crew numbers. But Bodega was not fazed. "For the King's service and the honour of the nation," he argued, the ship must sail on. Still not convinced, for many of the crew were affected by scurvy and it was already mid-July, Hezeta reluctantly agreed and assigned six men from the *Santiago* to the *Sonora*.

The end of July approached. On the night of July 29, well out from land, strong winds and high waves separated the ships. It was so dark that those on board the *Sonora* could not see even the rockets from the *Santiago*. Come morning, the frigate was not in sight. Bodega searched for his companion ship for three days, then continued north, "taking fresh trouble for granted."

How hard did Bodega and Mourelle look for the *Santiago*? Perhaps not very hard at all, for Mourelle later confessed the separation had been intentional. Hezeta was clearly leaning toward going home, and they did not think they could continue to carry the day against the wishes of their commanding officer. And they had no desire whatever to turn back—although all their jerked meat was stored on the *Santiago* and all they had was rice, beans, soggy bread, lard, and water; they had no medicines, and the *Sonora* was a pig of a ship; and, if they eventually returned with no glorious results, they could be accused of insubordination—yet, the glory of Spain and their own ambitions demanded that they fulfill their mission. As Mourelle later wrote, they were "two youths eager for fame and reputation." And such was

Bodega's talent for leadership that he was able to persuade his men that this was the best course for them to take.

Even their knowledge and up-to-date navigational instruments could not provide them with much certainty, but, on August 15, they saw signs of land again at what was probably just north of latitude 56° north. Escaping the thick fog, they sighted the coast the next day, drew in toward Kruzof Island and then entered an inlet between high snow-capped mountains.

They found a harbour three days later at the north end of the island. Bodega disembarked with fourteen well-armed men and took possession of the land for Spain. They desperately needed to take on fresh water, but the incident on the Olympic Peninsula had made them wary. Bodega fortified a point on land with swivel guns and men, then filled his water barrels and cut wood. All went well until the Natives saw the Spaniards carrying the water to their ship and insisted the Spanish must pay for this water, since it belonged to the occupants of the land. Faced with Bodega's guns, the Natives withdrew, but, as soon as the Spaniards left, they took down the cross and re-erected it in front of their village.

The fog drew in again, rain fell in torrents, and the weather turned yet colder. On August 22, they reached latitude 57° 58′ north. Though he wanted to sail on, Bodega realized the season was too far advanced, the ship too plagued with problems, and the men too ill. "Having many times been urged to return and not to endanger myself, I never abandoned my purpose until compelled to do so," he later wrote. Mourelle, though, still wanted to continue but reluctantly agreed to Bodega's decision.

Now they sailed south, as close as they could to land, seeking to chart the coastline and search for de Fonte's reputed passage to the Atlantic. Bodega did discover a well-protected harbour on Prince of Wales Island, which he named Entrada de Bucareli, for the viceroy. The bay provided the safety he required, and he wanted to stay longer to stock up on firewood and water, but time was too short. Soon, though, the winds changed. Tacking off the coast, they finally got westerly winds that carried them away from dangerous waters and rocks. Ever reluctant to give up, Bodega made one last attempt to turn back north, but, with most of his crew crippled by scurvy, this too had to be abandoned.

The North Pacific had still more to show them. On the night of September 6, heavy seas swamped the *Sonora*, panicking the crew and "tearing out railings, stanchions, clamps, and the gunwales of the deck house" and taking off everything that was on deck. Finally, the water began to drain away, leaving several crew members injured. Only Bodega, Mourelle, two seamen, a mate, and a servant were fit enough to crew the ship.

Though water still flooded into the hold, they somehow managed to run before the wind. All feared the ship would sink. With Bodega and Mourelle alternately handling the sails and manning the bilge pump, somehow it stayed afloat, though badly damaged. Wrote Mourelle, "[we] resolved to undertake this labor which in no ways conformed to [our] past exercise, and which could only have been withstood by two youths who sought heroism."

As they continued south, they could no longer manage to follow the shore. On September 17, they were off the entrance to Juan de Fuca Strait but could not get close. They searched for but did not find the Rio de Martin Aguilar and concluded it did not exist. Bodega and Mourelle had joined the ranks of the scurvy- and fever-ridden; the crew were in disarray. But as the weather improved, so did the spirits and bodies of the men.

Finally, they reached San Francisco Bay, but, with the launch lost to violent waves the night before, did not try to enter. On October 7, they entered the harbour at Monterey, to the great joy of the men aboard the *San Carlos* and the *Santiago*, anchored in the bay for the previous five weeks, who had given them up for lost. Not a member of *Sonora*'s crew could walk off the ship; all had to be helped ashore.

Eating well from the mission gardens and farm and enjoying the warmer climate, captain and crew recovered in the three weeks they stayed at Monterey. Hezeta told them he had searched for them after their separation for almost two weeks, then concluded the ship had sunk. Turning south, he had seen the entrance to the Columbia River and thought it might be "the mouth of some great river or some passage to another sea." Perhaps it might be Juan de Fuca's fabled strait, for he had seen no signs of that entrance at the latitude claimed by the Greek pilot. He then returned to Monterey.

Hezeta called another junta. He wanted to spend the winter in San Diego Bay and head north again the next spring. But the officers agreed that they must restore the ships, rest the men, and prepare properly for a new expedition. They arrived back at San Blas on November 20, minus Juan Pérez, who died en route, probably of typhoid fever. He was buried at sea with a mass and salute.

Was Bodega's decision to head north alone justified by the results of his voyage? And did the expedition accomplish any of its aims? Viceroy Bucareli thought so. He wrote to Madrid, praising the "gallant zeal" shown by Bodega and his "heroic constancy and disdain of risks," and commending Mourelle as well. King Carlos III was equally content: he ordered that the results of the expedition be officially published, though for Spanish eyes only, and that all the officers and pilots concerned be promoted. A new expedition was to be prepared, and Bodega was to command one of the ships. That expedition could make good use of all the charts and maps prepared in 1775.

The king and the viceroy were now even more determined that Spain must continue its quest for possession of the Northwest Coast. If there did exist a northwest passage, then it must be the Spaniards who found it.

4

Seeking Captain Cook

BODEGA'S AND MOURELLE'S HEROICS LEFT a central question unanswered: was there a passage from Atlantic to Pacific through, or north of, North America? The British Parliament certainly hoped so. Nothing could be more helpful to British commercial and imperial ambitions than a way to the west that avoided the treacherous and Spanish-controlled Strait of Magellan. After decades of discussion and the funding of various tentative expeditions to the north, Parliament decided to offer a strong incentive. In 1774, it put forward a reward of £20,000 to the first British merchant ship to successfully navigate the long-sought passage. Two years later, it extended the offer to ships of the British navy and their captains.

The Admiralty, in command of the navy, was intrigued. The First Lord of the Admiralty thought Captain James Cook, a twenty-year veteran of the navy who had already made two stellar voyages along the southern route around the world, was the perfect person to lead an exploring expedition into the northern seas. Cook, ever the adventurer, was eager for more success and more fame. Somehow, through theft, bribery, or espionage, a copy of the journal and maps Mourelle had prepared after the *Sonora*'s 1775 voyage made its way to Britain and was translated into English. Mourelle's words and charts would be of great assistance to the British sea commander.

Cook and his two ships, the *Resolution* and *Discovery*, left Plymouth early in 1776, ostensibly bound for Tahiti but in reality headed, eventually, for the Northwest Coast. On his two-year voyage, before his untimely death in the Hawaiian Islands, Cook had reached the Oregon coast, then arrived at Nootka Sound, where he named the cove that fronted the Nuu-chah-nulth village of Yuquot, Friendly Cove, for the amicable reception he received there. He spent a month in Nootka Sound, then headed north, mapping what he could see of the coast as far as Bering Strait.

Spain's diplomats and spies brought home news of Cook's impending voyage. Breaking through the smoke-screen of the visit to Tahiti, they soon learned Cook's true purpose—the visit to the Northwest Coast and the search for a northwest passage. This, Spain, decided, they could not allow. In 1692, Madrid had passed a law that, unless they received advance permission for any voyages into Spain's claimed territory along the Pacific coast, foreign sailors were to be treated as enemies. Still remembering Francis Drake and other English privateers, Spain was particularly opposed to any British activity in the region. British traders were notably aggressive, and Spain feared their effect on the thinly fortified Spanish colonies on the west coast of the Americas. Firm supporters of a mercantilist doctrine, Spain maintained close control over her colonies, forbidding any trade with other nations, banning the export of gold and silver, and keeping watch on any foreign ships that might put into colonial ports. If Cook landed anywhere on the Northwest Coast, he would undoubtedly claim the land for Britain, something Spain could not countenance. Heaven forbid that he should discover a northwest passage, for then Spain's commerce and claims would lie in rags.

The Spanish crown issued orders: if Cook was found anywhere on the coast claimed by Spain, he should be refused all aid and supplies and hindered in all ways short of actual force.

This was easier said than done. Spain's resources were concentrated in what is now the southwest United States, Mexico, and the Caribbean, far from the ports of Acapulco and San Blas. Nonetheless, Madrid decided that more must be done to forestall Cook. In 1776, the minister in charge of New Spain ordered that an expedition be mounted to consolidate Spain's claims to the coast as far north as Russia's Alaskan colonies and to promote settlement and trade along the coast.

Viceroy Bucareli agreed that, ideally, ships should sail north to accomplish these aims. But which ships and with which men? Bodega and Mourelle had sailed north in a manifestly unsuitable ship and had been lucky to survive and return. It would be foolishness to send a new expedition even farther north, charged with charting dangerous passages, unless they had more suitable ships and better support. Five ships were headquartered at San Blas. One was under repair, and four were taking supplies to the missions in California. Bucareli wrote to Madrid that he lacked the iron to have more ships built, that it would be difficult to bring cannons overland from the Caribbean to arm the ships, and that he did not have the resources to outfit any new ships. It was more important to expand and reinforce the settlements in California. With reluctance, Bucareli told Madrid he could not do as commanded.

His response was not well received in Madrid. The minister in charge commanded that Bucareli must mount an expedition; if his men found Cook, they must arrest him and take over his ships.

Frustrated by Spain's lack of understanding, Bucareli complied half-heartedly. Learning of the weak response, the minister in Madrid was not amused. He ordered that adequate ships be found or built in Callao, Peru, and sailed north to Mexico. Bodega was sent to Peru to acquire such a ship.

In Bodega's opinion, none of the navy's ships at Callao could withstand the wind and waves of the north coast. He heard, though, that a merchant ship called the *Favorita* was on its way from Chile, and he thought it might serve the purpose. When she finally drew into port three months later, he persuaded the owner to sell her, and began rebuilding the ship to suit his purposes. Two and a half months later, he had the ship he wanted, converted to a frigate, armed, with good storage space and improved strength to withstand northwestern weather. The *Favorita* had for a figurehead a mermaid; not suitable, declared Bodega, and had a lion installed on the prow.

Bodega and the *Favorita* left Callao in late December 1777, arriving at San Blas in February 1778. Ship workers were toiling there on the *Princesa*, a frigate similar to the *Favorita*. The expedition would not be able to leave for the Northwest until 1779. In the meantime, some thorny questions had to be answered. Bodega had done a fine job on the 1775 expedition, and it seemed logical to appoint him to head the next voyage; the king expressed the wish that this should happen. But Bodega, promoted for his good service and now a *teniente de navio* (lieutenant), had less seniority at that rank than other officers at San Blas. Could he be appointed over more senior officers?

The senior officer at San Blas was under a cloud. Ignacio de Arteaga y Bazan had spent three years in a Spanish naval prison for trying to marry without the necessary permission and had insulted the ecclesiastical tribunal that had reviewed his case. Released in 1774, he had been sent to San Blas as something of a punishment. Though he had no experience on the coast, he did have seniority, and Bucareli had to select him as overall commander of the expedition and captain of the *Princesa*. Then Bucareli named Bodega as captain of the *Favorita*, with Mourelle as second-in-command.

As carpenters and shipwrights hammered away at the *Princesa*, Bodega and Arteaga carefully planned their expedition. They decided to sail directly to Bucareli Bay, rather than stopping at any of the California missions. They agreed that if the ships were separated at sea, they would meet at the bay, then follow the coast to at least latitude 65° north, taking possession wherever they could land as far north as they could reach. Once they turned back south, they would explore the bays and inlets along the way back to San Diego. They would carry stores sufficient for fifteen months and fresh water enough for eight. Each of the 205 men would be issued a *quartillo* of wine—about 200 millilitres—per day as a preventative against scurvy.

Each ship would carry charts and maps, trade goods, surveying and astronomical instruments, medicines, extra clothing against the cold of the north, several barrels of brandy, and candles to be used in religious observances.

Between them, they would be armed with fourteen cannons and fifteen swivel guns, and with sufficient pistols, ammunition, and swords to make a brave show against any aggressor.

The expedition left San Blas on February 12, 1779. The wind was not favourable, and, almost becalmed, they could travel only five nautical miles in two days. Sweating in the heat and humidity, the crew made quick inroads into the barrels of fresh water. Bodega and Mourelle were less than impressed by the decisions of Arteaga, a novice at this kind of sailing, but the two ships finally sailed into open ocean more or less together, though Bodega had to shorten sail not to outrun the slower *Princesa*. Once the ships were at sea, the winds blew them north at a steady pace and they gained more than fifty nautical miles each day.

This smooth and steady progress was interrupted when the winds howled at gale force in early April and waves flooded over the decks. Tossed on the heavy seas, the *Princesa* was the worse affected, as all the deck cargo was thrown into chaos, the medicine chest upended, and most of its contents lost overboard. The gale abated, and two weeks later, the ships crossed the Tropic of Cancer. Off northern California, a new fierce storm separated the two ships. Arteaga and the priest aboard the *Princesa* pleaded with Our Lady to deliver them from the storm, and shortly thereafter, the seas calmed. But the *Favorita* was nowhere in sight, and, independently, the two captains decided to proceed separately, as agreed, to Bucareli Bay.

Late in April, the crew of the *Favorita* began to see kelp, ducks, sea lions, sea otters, and other signs of land. On the morning of May 1, they caught sight of the snowy hills and mountains that lay behind Bucareli Bay. After eighty-two days at sea, the *Favorita* entered the bay and let down its anchor. Amazingly, the *Princesa* entered the bay that same afternoon. After trying several different anchorages, they agreed on a place they named Puerto Santa Cruz.

Extremely pleased with this anchorage, Arteaga and Bodega decided to explore the country and coast nearby. A landing party nailed a cross almost five metres wide to the trunk of a tree they had cut down, and the ships fired their guns in a salute, thus claiming the land for king, country, and God. A crowd of Native people watched this solemn ceremony. The Spaniards then began collecting firewood and fresh water, loaded aboard rocks as ballast, and repaired damage caused by the long voyage.

With Mourelle in command, the two ships' launches set out, powered by triangular sails and oars and towing a canoe bought from First Nations people, either Tlingit or Kaigani Haida. At night, they went ashore to prepare meals and sleep under the sails. All the while, they charted the shores and made note of the villages, clothing, and customs. Though the relationship seemed mostly friendly, some uneasy moments occurred. Clearly testing Spanish resolve, at one point a crowd of Native people arrived by canoe, yelling and gesturing with daggers and spears at the

Spaniards on the beach. But, "as it was never our intention to do them any harm, in spite of having suffered so many impertinences and taunts . . . we all withdrew quickly and with stealth to the launches, together with our big cooking pot and half-cooked supper."

Some three hundred men in twenty-three canoes followed the launches from now on, and Mourelle finally decided he had to make some gesture. As a demonstration of firepower, he fired his guns at the towed canoe and at the trees. It did not work; that night, Natives stole the sails over the pilots' shelter. A larger and more convincing gesture was needed. Mourelle ordered a group to go ashore, where they captured a hostage and held him against the return of the sails and other items. The sails had been torn apart, and nothing else recovered, so Mourelle ordered the hostage be given forty lashes and set free. He also fired his swivel guns into the woods as a warning. Oddly, the encounters resumed in relative peace. Mourelle, however, continued to write of the Natives' "insufferable arrogance."

The launches were out for almost a month. Meanwhile, back at the frigates, many of those aboard the *Princesa*, including Arteaga, fell ill, possibly with food poisoning, and several died. The illness conquered, they resumed wooding and watering, repairing and cleaning both ship and clothes—an activity Bodega insisted on to maintain health.

The Natives then gave the Spaniards dried fish, woven mats, sea otter and seal pelts, and bear and deer skins, seeking pieces of iron and copper in return. Bodega and Arteaga were concerned about some overt displays of hostility, and rumours reached them of an impending attack. When the Natives pulled down the cross to remove the iron nails, the Spaniards fired their cannons and sent crew members ashore to collect the pieces of the cross. Then a number of the offenders apologized, and the Spanish were able to erect another cross. With everyone content, the launches returned.

As the captains prepared to depart, more hostilities occurred between the Spanish and Native people. Eventually, though, the ships set sail from Bucareli Bay, carrying with them five Native children who had been offered to them. Though overlong, the Spaniards' two months at the bay had been pleasant. Now they must once more sail into cold, rain, and some degree of misery. Light winds and fog delayed their progress, but after nineteen days, they reached the entrance to Prince William Sound, just north of latitude 60°, tucked at the north end of the Kenai Peninsula and east of present-day Anchorage. They named the port at its entrance Santiago. Here they made another formal act of possession, the farthest north point where Spain was ever to perform such a ceremony.

On they went through the long northern days, but a storm blew up, driving the ships before it until they could finally find shelter. One more ceremony of possession was performed, but the rains fell heavily now. Some seven men had died of scurvy and other ailments, many of the crew were ill, and more were falling ill every day "because of the unremitting rains and excessive cold." Arteaga decided they had done what they had set out to do and could now turn back south for home. They had not, he noted, encountered "any passage to the north to climb to latitude 70°." And though he did not confess it until later, he was very ill himself, with a paralysis that prevented him from doing anything.

Predictably, Bodega and Mourelle were not happy. "Such hardships are usual in such navigations," Bodega later wrote. "We had stores in abundance." Mourelle was even more direct: "The commandant should have taken advantage of the best part of the season which remained to reconnoitre the coast to the south . . . [We] were equipped with two beautiful ships for the purpose, ample stores, well supplied and well manned . . . But [the] determination to return rendered fruitless the terrible costs incurred by the Royal Treasury and the most notable care taken by His Excellency Viceroy Bucareli to ensure that nothing required was lacking."

This time, though, they had to hew to the commanding officer's decision. The two frigates sailed south, losing contact once more and reuniting at San Francisco Bay on September 14.

Seventeen of the returning sailors were ill with scurvy and other ailments when they arrived. All on board the two ships were weary. What a relief it was to move onto shore and feast on the fresh vegetables and meat the mission gardens and farm offered. The priests were kind, the weather was warm and dry, and the men no longer had to cope with the constant uncertainty and heaving decks of the tiny ships. Not surprisingly, the captains elected to remain in San Francisco for five weeks, recuperating, writing journals, and completing maps of their journey.

They also caught up on the news. Totally without outside contact for the seven months of their voyage, they did not know that Viceroy Bucareli, the strong supporter of exploring the Northwest Coast, had died just two months after they had left San Blas. Nor were they aware that Spain had joined with France to support the rebelling British colonies in North America, thus deepening the hostility and rivalry between Britain and Spain. And they had no idea that their mission of pursuing and possibly arresting Captain James Cook had been rendered meaningless. Cook had reached the Northwest Coast in 1778, long before they had even set sail. Two days after the Spaniards left San Blas on their mission, Cook was stabbed to death in Hawaii. British captain Charles Clerke took over the mission and made one more attempt to find a northwest passage. Beset by the symptoms of tuberculosis he had contracted in a debtors' prison in England, he, too, died as the ships sailed from Bering Strait to Kamchatka. The ships then returned to Britain.

Leaving the San Francisco mission, Arteaga and Bodega sailed out into the ocean once more, only to be immediately engulfed in thick fog. Separately, they made their way south. In late November, they arrived back at San Blas, after a journey of some 9,500 nautical miles. The two captains sent off their reports. Despite illness and adversity, they said, they had done all they could to advance knowledge of the Northwest Coast and to reinforce Spain's claim to the region.

Both asked for various promotions for their officers, praising them strongly. And Arteaga had one more favour to request: he had married without permission, as the king well knew, but perhaps his wife and children might nonetheless receive his pension in the event of his death—a request that was subsequently granted.

What now for the Spanish in the Northwest? The Spanish hierarchy needed to evaluate the voyage and decide on further explorations. In general, the home government expressed its pleasure. Since Arteaga and Bodega had not investigated the reports that foreign ships were sailing the Northwest Coast, Madrid was satisfied that no threats existed to its control of the Pacific coast. The glory of Spain seemed not to be at risk.

It was a shame that no time or effort had been spent on converting the Natives on the coast, but God could well be served on voyages and settlements in the future, when time and resources allowed. As for gain, they had found no riches. The explorers had found no evidence of a northwest passage and had not filled in the chart of the coast from Bucareli Bay south to San Francisco. The voyage had been extremely expensive, and the results seemed slim.

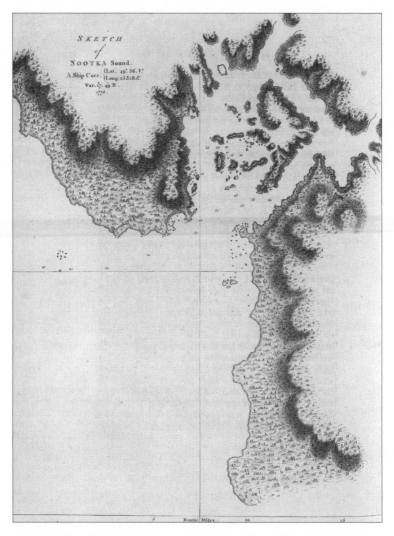

A detailed map of Nootka Sound drawn by crew members who voyaged with Captain James Cook in 1778.

Once more, Spain needed to focus elsewhere. It had been forced to cede Florida to the British in return for Havana and Cuba; Madrid would like to gain that colony back. Trade between Acapulco and the Philippines was a priority, and Manila must be forcefully defended. Spain wanted to reclaim Gibraltar and needed to defend the Rio de la Plata region at Buenos Aires. In 1780, considering expense, time, and desire, the Spanish king ordered that expeditions to the Northwest Coast cease. Spanish naval officers, including Bodega, were reassigned to Havana or Manila, and the San Blas forces reduced by half. For another decade, Spanish endeavours would reach no farther north than the California missions.

5

A Quarrelsome Man

BUSY ELSEWHERE, SPAIN MIGHT HAVE preferred to continue to ignore the Northwest Coast. By joining the fight against Britain in the American Revolution, however, Madrid had ensured that Britain and British traders would challenge Spanish claims elsewhere. Perhaps, said some Britons, they could weaken Spain by joining with Russia to take over the Northwest Coast. Such an incursion would have great commercial results. Though neither gold nor silver nor other riches had been found on the land, the luxurious pelts of the sea otter were almost as precious. Beaver skins underlay expansion across the Canadian wilderness, and sable pelts financed Russian expansion across Siberia. But a sea otter skin was worth at least twenty times the price of a sable pelt, ten times that of a beaver.

Russian traders had sailed on from the Aleutians to Unalaska and the Alaska Panhandle. They were not the only interlopers on the coast. Some twenty American and British traders arrived at Nootka between 1785 and 1788. Spain was poorly placed to compete with the Russians and British. Some Spanish merchants tried to work a triangular trade, taking furs from the coast to Manila and returning with quicksilver (mercury) needed to refine the gold of the South American mines. But restrictive trading policies and petty bickering among rival companies wanting to preserve a monopoly in Manila often scuttled trading efforts.

Was it possible that Spain could lose the entire region to foreign interests? Rumour and report gathered from Spanish ports and foreign courts suggested the threat was real. Estéban José Martinez, a pilot based out of San Blas, was on a supply mission to San Francisco one day in 1786 when he espied the ship of French explorer Jean-François de Galaup, usually known as the Count of Lapérouse. Lapérouse was on a round-the-world expedition at the behest of King Louis XVI. Since the French and Spanish were allies, Martinez piloted Lapérouse's ship into the bay, and asked for a report on the voyage. Somehow, he gained the idea that the Russians had sailed down the coast and erected a post at Nootka. Disturbed, he sent a message to the viceroy at Mexico City.

His was not the only warning. Spanish ambassadors

to the Russian court also reported that Russia was moving south along the coast and intended to build permanent posts wherever they could reach. Not to be permitted, said Madrid, and ordered an expedition sent out immediately from San Blas to investigate.

Where were the ships and men to come from? The commanders of previous expeditions, such as Bodega and Arteaga, were elsewhere, in the Caribbean, the Mediterranean, or Manila. The only experienced officer available was Martinez, who went with Pérez as second pilot in 1774. His performance had met with mixed reviews, and he was not sent on the 1775 voyage. Despite his drawbacks, he was the ranking officer at San Blas, so was named to head the expedition and captain the ship *Princesa*. Gonzales Lopez de Haro was to captain the expedition's second ship, the *San Carlos*. Each captain had two pilots, officers, and crew on board.

The royal instructions directed the expedition to sail north at least as far as 61° and investigate any Russian settlements they came across, discovering how many people were at each and whether they were permanent or temporary. This voyage was to be one of reconnaissance only: the leaders were not to dispute with any Russians they found. The expedition should also seek good harbours and suitable locations to acquire wood and fresh water, as well as investigate the possibilities of establishing gardens and growing crops. If possible, they should bring back one person from each First Nation they encountered, to be trained as interpreters for future voyages.

A Quarrelsome Man

Setting out from San Blas in March 1788, the ships arrived off Prince William Sound in early May. Martinez was in a quarrelsome mood. He declared an island ahead of the ships was the Isla del Carmen, noted on Spain's 1779 charts. Pilot Antonio Serantes thought it was a different island, one noted on Cook's charts. Martinez demanded that Serantes alter his log so it agreed with his; all the other officers agreed with Serantes. Thoroughly aggrieved and probably not sure of where he was, Martinez refused to enter the sound, keeping the ships hanging about at its entrance. Martinez, Haro later wrote, "with his loud language and bad behaviour, had reduced everything to so much foolishness, without taking any resolute action from one day to the next . . . We navigated in such a disjointed fashion . . . [that] a good many days were lost." To add to his officers' irritation, he ordered them to enter false courses and winds in their logs to justify his indecision.

Serantes at first agreed to do so, then changed his mind. Furious, Martinez slapped Serantes in the face and knocked him down. He then had him arrested and sent him to the *San Carlos*. Haro, on the *San Carlos*, did not agree with the arrest but kept Serantes on his ship, out of Martinez's way though not imprisoned. What was Martinez's problem? Serantes thought he knew. "Every time the said Don Estéban Martinez got intoxicated, for frequently he had more than one drink," he behaved badly.

Sober, Martinez was semi-apologetic, but Haro had had

enough of the inactivity. Although ordered to keep in sight of the *Princesa*, he took the *San Carlos* off northwest toward Unalaska Island in the Aleutians, where the ships were to rendezvous. On the shore of the Kenai Peninsula, he made contact with Natives who showed him vouchers in Russian writing received in trade for sea otter furs. At Three Saints Bay on Kodiak Island, a Russian boat came out to meet them, and Haro went ashore for lunch. Evstrat Delarov informed him that no Russian was yet at Nootka, but that next year, they planned to send several ships there from Siberia. The Russians, said Delarov, already had seven posts on the coast— an exaggeration, but one Haro could not disprove.

Martinez and the *Princesa*, meanwhile, continued up the coast, arriving at Dutch Harbor in Unalaska, where he, too, was told the Russians were going to Nootka the following year to keep the English out. Cook's account of his voyage had worried the Russians as much as it had concerned the Spanish. The *Princesa* stayed here for several weeks, with Martinez enjoying Russian hospitality and vodka. When Haro arrived, Martinez had harsh words for him and declared that all pilots were worthless and he would punish them if he could. Haro suggested in a later letter that Martinez was drunk yet again and was disobeying orders by carousing with the Russian trader.

Still furious, Martinez relieved Haro of his command, but when all the officers begged him not to do this, he did not follow through. His temper did not improve, however.

"At each moment, he became more and more inflamed," threatening to sink the *San Carlos*, Haro reported. The officers could protest his conduct all they liked when they all returned to San Blas, declaimed Martinez, but "neither money, gifts nor laws could beat him." He hinted that he would destroy any logs that did not agree with his own, that he would arrest Haro if he dissented, and that he would deal harshly with anyone who wrote about any of this to the viceroy. He told Haro he had just wasted his time at the Russian posts, since Martinez had already discovered everything there was to know about the Russians. Haro, however, had already discerned that most of what they had been told about Russian expansion was untrue.

Argument, dissension, and delay were rendering the expedition ineffective, and it was clearly time to head home. Some of the officers went ashore on August 5, surreptitiously, lest the Russians see what they were up to, and performed a short ceremony, burying a bottle containing their possession document. Ten days later, the ships headed south. Haro and the *San Carlos*, bedevilled by contrary winds and fog, were soon out of sight of the *Princesa*. Instructed to keep visual contact all the way home and if separated to meet up at Monterey, the officers of the ship held a junta to decide what to do. It was too late in the season to chart the coast, and they were fed up with Martinez. Disobeying his orders, they decided to head directly to San Blas.

Martinez arrived at Monterey and settled in to wait for

the *San Carlos*. When it had not arrived after a month, he sailed for San Blas, where he found Haro in residence. The *San Carlos* officers had already sent their version of the dispute to the viceroy. Furious but pre-empted, Martinez now wrote his own considerably different account, omitting all mention of any disagreements. The viceroy, Manuel Flores, was dubious of both accounts. He was more concerned by Martinez's report that four Russian frigates would arrive at Nootka in 1789, and he made a strong recommendation to Madrid that Spain must occupy Nootka before the Russians arrived.

He perceived that the threat to Spanish interests was not one to king and commerce alone. If the Russians succeeded in converting the First Nations of the coast to the Russian Orthodox faith, their very souls would be in danger. Furthermore, the entry of the Russians into the North Pacific would presumably be followed by their sailing farther south, and Spain's trade with Manila and China would be equally at risk. First the sea otters, then the souls; the Russians must be forestalled.

Madrid agreed that Spain must hasten to Nootka and plant a settlement there to back up the country's claims of possession on the Northwest Coast. We will send troops and priests, settlers, and cattle, said Flores. We will chart the whole coast from San Francisco to Cook Inlet. Flores keenly regretted the lack of better officers of higher rank and with more skills at San Blas, leaving him little choice as to who would command the new expedition. Martinez was very willing to lead it, "sacrificing my last breath in the service of God and the king." Flores decreed that the officers who had gone on the 1788 voyage must return together in 1789, putting aside all thought of the disputes that had occurred.

The instructions were plain. The expedition should sail directly to Nootka. Once there, the men should make as if they were building a permanent settlement, with a shed as a barracks and a place to meet with the Natives, plus a trench for defence and gardens to help feed the men. The men should not sleep onshore, but at night return to the ships. If the Russians or English were to arrive, the Spaniards should be civil, but tell them Spain possessed this land by right of prior discovery and present settlement. As proof, Flores cited the two silver spoons Cook had bought from the Nuu-chah-nulth, who had pilfered them from the 1774 Spanish expedition. If foreigners should use force to try to land, "you will repel it as far as your own strength permits." Further, they were to prevent any such foreigners from trading with the Natives.

If by any chance American ships should arrive, Martinez could take whatever measures he thought appropriate. The *San Carlos* should be sent north to explore back from 55° to Nootka and take formal possession wherever possible.

Turmoil at Nootka

WHAT WAS THE ENGLISH CAPTAIN of the *Argonaut* up to at Nootka Sound? Estéban Martinez suspected the worst: James Colnett had not been honest with him and had refused to produce his orders. On board his ship *Princesa*, Martinez challenged Colnett. Colnett replied with all the arrogance he was capable of, which proved to be a great deal. The argument escalated. Don't you dare question or detain me, Colnett shouted, his hand on the hilt of his sword. Do your worst, fire on my ship: I do not fear you. The Englishman cursed Spain, and Martinez erupted. A clutch of soldiers entered the cabin and took Colnett prisoner. Hours later, Spanish soldiers commandeered the *Argonaut*.

The scene at Nootka in 1789 threw the usually peaceful Northwest Coast into turmoil and almost led to war between Spain and Britain. It came in the midst of five years of unparalleled Spanish activity on the coast, following a decade of that country's absence. Martinez on the *Princesa* and Haro on the *San Carlos* had left San Blas in mid-February of 1789, together with 4 Franciscans charged with converting the First Nations people, 28 soldiers, and a crew of 164. The *Princesa* reached Nootka on May 2, the *San Carlos* on May 12. Just off Nootka, Martinez encountered Robert Gray, an American fur trader captaining the sloop *Lady Washington*. Gray and his fellow American captain, John Kendrick, aboard the *Columbia Rediviva*, had spent the winter at Nootka, trading for all the sea otter pelts the Nuu-chah-nulth had to offer. Martinez fired a shot across the sloop's bows and asked that her captain come aboard. Instead, Gray sent two officers. The talk was relatively cordial. Gray told Martinez the ship *Ifigenia Nubiana* was anchored at Nootka, with captain William Douglas claiming it was of Portuguese registry. But, said Gray, the captain and crew were English and the Portuguese registry a fiction, a way of getting around trade restrictions the British had imposed on British-registered ships. Then the *Lady Washington* headed off north, while Martinez continued into harbour.

The *Ifigenia Nubiana* had been at Nootka since mid-April, part of an ambitious effort by British merchant captain John Meares both to trade for sea otter furs on the Northwest Coast and to claim Nootka for the British. Meares had first reached the Alaskan coast in 1786; he arrived at Nootka in 1788 with two ships, including the *Ifigenia*. He later claimed he had bought all of the land around Friendly Cove from the Nuu-chah-nulth chief Maquinna. Whatever the truth of his claim, he built a habitation there, either a rough shack or a large dwelling, depending on whom you believe. His men also built a small ship, the *Northwest America*.

When Martinez arrived at Nootka, he was unaware of Meares's grandiose plans, but if the *Ifigenia* was indeed British, a confrontation was inevitable. He went ashore, where he was given a traditional welcome by the Nuu-chah-nulth. The next day, many canoes came alongside, seeking abalone shells and copper sheets in return for fish, plants, and furs. Over the following few weeks, the Spaniards started work on a fort on San Miguel Island, at the entrance to the cove, to protect the settlement they named Santa Cruz de Nuca. They also erected three buildings, a forge, and a bake oven, and began a vegetable garden. Martinez, meanwhile, considered how to deal with the *Ifigenia*.

The ship carried papers in Portuguese that ordered her captain and crew to take possession of any Russian, Spanish, or British ship that attacked her and bring ship and crew to Macao, where they would be condemned as pirates. Also aboard were secret orders in English to take possession of the region. Douglas refused to show these latter papers to Martinez, but the Spaniard was convinced that the interlopers were paying no heed to Spanish claims to the coast. Charging the ship and its captain with having violated Spanish sovereignty, he arrested Douglas and, on May 13, seized the *Ifigenia*, hoisted the Spanish flag on it, and transferred all its armaments to the *Princesa*. Finding it in bad condition, he had the ship caulked and the sails repaired. He permitted the ship to depart when Douglas promised—probably with fingers crossed—not to return or to trade along the coast. It was, after all, a big ocean and a long coast, and Spanish resources were limited. Despite the often acrimonious dispute, Spanish, English, and American captains had a farewell dinner aboard the *Princesa*.

On June 8, the *Northwest America* arrived, and Martinez, again relying on his interpretation of the viceroy's orders, seized her. She was then recaulked, repaired, and rechristened the *Santa Gertrudis la Magna*, and used by Martinez to further explore the coast. When another of Meares's ships, the *Princess Royal*, captained by Thomas Hudson, arrived on June 15, he left her free, since Hudson said the ship entered harbour under distress. Hudson took his ship out again on July 2, claiming he was going to China.

On June 24, the Spanish undertook a very elaborate ceremony of possession for King Carlos III, showing the flag to all who might challenge Spanish claims. With sword drawn, Martinez cut branches, moved stones, and made other

The friendship of Nuu-chah-nulth chief Maquinna was key to Spanish interests at Friendly Cove. The cove and Nootka Sound lay within Maquinna's traditional territory.

DAVID RUMSEY MAP COLLECTION, WWW.DAVIDRUMSEY.COM

physical moves intended to demonstrate that no one, British or American, challenged his right to do so. The men erected a giant cross and buried a bottle containing documents of possession. Cannonades and volleys followed; the crew shouted "*Viva el Rey*" seven times from on board, answered by volleys from on shore. The ceremony was followed by a great feast to which the American and British officers were invited. To reinforce the Spanish claim, Maquinna was asked to describe the banner that flew from the first European ship to visit Nootka. Unhesitatingly, he described the Spanish naval banner.

On July 2, another British ship sailed into harbour. The *Argonaut*'s captain, James Colnett, was just as irascible and short-tempered as Martinez. Both would rue the day they met, and Colnett would become a considerable thorn in Spain's side. Colnett declared his ship was owned by the United Company of Merchants of England, another name for the East India Company. He had, said Colnett, been appointed governor of Nootka Sound by the king of England. Martinez begged to differ. Colnett said the whole coast belonged to Britain because James Cook had claimed it. Martinez said that the Spanish had been there more than three years before Cook. With no agreement reached, Martinez had the *Argonaut* towed into harbour, refusing Colnett permission to erect any structure.

The following morning, Martinez invited Colnett aboard the *Princesa*, asking him to bring with him the papers of his ship. They argued; Colnett, Martinez later reported, placed his hand on his sword and shouted "the evil-sounding and denigrating words '*Gardem España*' [Goddamn Spain]." Such insults were not to be countenanced; the following day, Martinez had Colnett arrested and took the *Argonaut* under charge.

This inflammatory illustration is captioned as "The Spanish Insult to the British Flag at Nootka Sound." Published in the British press, it was used to rally support for the idea that Britain should go to war with Spain over Nootka after Martinez seized ships belonging to Meares. Martinez is shown orchestrating the arrest of Colnett and the seizure of the *Argonaut* as his unprepossessing men look on and the Spanish ships loom large over the stalwart Briton. Unmentioned is the fact that there was no British flag flying on the *Argonaut*. Sentiment was so strong that a pantomime based on the incident played to large crowds at London's Covent Garden in 1790. LIBRARY OF CONGRESS

Spaniards and Americans at Nootka were still good friends, and on July 4, cannonades and salutes boomed across the little bay. Colnett, confined to shipboard, was not amused. His second-in-command reported his state of mind: "Captain Colnett has been in a high state of insanity; sometimes he starts, at other times he asks how long he has to live, who is to be his executioner, what death he is to be put to, with all such delirious expressions . . . which induces me and every other person who sees him, to believe his brain is turned."

Martinez's patience had been sorely tried and his limited capacity for peaceful diplomacy exhausted. When Hudson returned aboard the *Princess Royal*, having broken his word and continued trading despite his promise to go to China, he and the *Princess Royal* were also arrested. Martinez threatened to put Hudson and some of his men to the sword if they resisted arrest and to hang Colnett and Hudson if necessary. Was it a bluff, or was the threat real? Martinez later claimed it a bluff, but the threat would not play well in later negotiations between the nations.

The dispute led to another with serious consequences. Some of the *Argonaut*'s crew members were allowed ashore, where they tried to foment trouble by talking to Maquinna. Callicum, Maquinna's relative, decided to take a hand in the discussions by going out to talk with Haro. Martinez saw Callicum leaving the *San Carlos* and asked him to come aboard the *Princesa*. The chief was fonder of the English than of the Spanish and cursed Martinez as a rogue and thief, calling him down for his seizure of the English ships. Exasperated by the tirade, Martinez seized a musket and fired it in the general direction of Callicum. The gun misfired, but a sailor thought Martinez was under attack, and shot and killed Callicum.

Spanish, English, and Nuu-chah-nulth alike were shocked and saddened by the death. When Callicum's relatives wanted to retrieve his body, the Spanish foolishly forced them to pay five sea otter skins for the privilege. The incident stained the relations between the Nuu-chah-nulth and Spanish for some time thereafter.

The seizure of the ships created a new problem for Martinez: how to feed the crews. The supply ship he expected to arrive from San Blas had not done so, and even when it did, it would not have sufficient to feed the captured and the garrison that was to overwinter at Nootka. He sent the *San Carlos* south to Monterey to pick up cattle, sheep, and all the other provisions that would be needed. The captured *Princess Royal* and crew would go south with the *San Carlos,* under Spanish captain José Maria Narváez, her armaments left behind to strengthen the Spanish defences.

7

Arresting Developments

JUST ONE DAY AFTER THE *San Carlos* sailed, the frigate *Nuestra Señora del Aranzazu* drew into harbour, carrying supplies for the Nootka Sound settlement. The captain also brought bad news for Martinez: he was ordered to abandon Nootka before the end of October. Martinez was aghast. With one instruction, the viceroy had rendered pointless all his actions of the summer. He would obey, he wrote to Flores, but reluctantly, for if Friendly Cove were left unoccupied, it would be ever more difficult for Madrid to maintain Spain's claim to the region.

The *San Carlos* did not return. Nor did new instructions arrive. Martinez proceeded to dismantle the shore works, burying the crates of brick and lime he had brought with him against what he saw as the certainty that Spain would return to build a settlement once more. To underline his view, when the small ship *Fair American* out of Macao arrived on October 6 with her cargo of furs obtained in Unalaska, he seized the ship. Martinez then went south with this ship, as well as the renamed *Santa Gertrudis la Magna* and the *Princesa*, arriving at San Blas on December 6. There he discovered that the communications time lag had struck again. On April 14, 1789, a good four months before the order to abandon reached Martinez, the king had ordered that the establishment at Nootka should be maintained "with honour and firmness." Martinez must have felt vindicated, if somewhat exasperated.

Much else had changed while Martinez was at Nootka. King Carlos III had died at the end of 1788 and was succeeded by his son, Carlos IV. The Conde de Revillagigedo had been named to replace Flores as viceroy. Bodega was instructed to return to San Blas as commandant of the post, taking with him six junior officers to bolster Spain's presence on the west coast. Revillagigedo and Bodega travelled together to Vera Cruz, where the new viceroy learned of the seizures and arrests at Nootka. The two hastened to Mexico City, where Flores was happy to hand over responsibility for the whole difficult situation. Bodega then made his way overland to San Blas, arriving late in December 1789. The *Fair American* was released on Revillagigedo's orders, and Bodega turned his attention to the problem of the English prisoners.

Already at San Blas since August, they had made their presence felt. The port was hot, humid, and disease-ridden. Eight of the prisoners had died there, including one who had committed suicide. Colnett, as was his wont, was fractious and disagreeable. They should never have been arrested, he declaimed; they certainly should not have to remain in such a miserable place—a point of view he shared with most of the Spaniards who lived at San Blas. The heat was horrendous, the mosquitoes unbearable, and he had to eat at the same table with his own officers, most of whom he disliked.

In November, the English officers were permitted to move to Tepic. Colnett wasn't much happier. Furious that the Spanish were using the *Argonaut* and had sent it to Acapulco, he sent missive after missive to Revillagigedo. Once Bodega arrived, he moderated his complaints, considering the officer an honourable man. But once he learned that the *Princess Royal*, now renamed the *Princesa Real*, was to sail back to Nootka under Spanish command, his indignation remounted to fever pitch. Bodega tried to calm him by replying that the viceroy had ordered the ship be used, but if it were damaged at all, it would be repaired and reparations would be paid when the ship was finally returned.

Colnett was further incensed when Bodega told him he would not be allowed to leave Mexico just yet. He could, however, travel to Mexico City to petition Revillagigedo for his release and that of his men and ships. The viceroy agreed to this, provided Colnett promised not to trade in Spanish ports or Spanish waters. Colnett had other grievances and demands, but by July 1790, the *Argonaut* was back in his hands. Never satisfied, he continued his complaints. The delay was insufferable, he said, and he differed with Bodega on what had become known as the Spanish Balance—the amount owing to Colnett after accounting for the use of his ships, provisions, supplies, and equipment, minus the supplies Bodega had placed aboard his ship and the expenses incurred in housing, clothing, and caring for him and his men at San Blas and Tepic.

At last, Bodega cracked. Calm and courteous to this point, he demanded that Colnett sign a letter saying he agreed with everything. Only then would he be permitted to depart. With little choice, Colnett signed and "sailed immediately and released myself from the tyranny, cruelty, [and] robbery of the inhabitants of New Spain."

Though it would continue to rankle with both sides, the drama at San Blas and Tepic was in some ways just a sideshow to the real issue. Existing relations between the two countries were testy at best. Still smarting over Spain's support for the breakaway American colonies and Spain's attempts to disrupt Britain's colonial empire, London had tried to return the favour. British prime minister William Pitt met with a Venezulan revolutionary and promised Britain's support for any South American attempts at independence. His agents were instructed to encourage rebellion in Mexico and North America, not because Britain wanted the colonies to go free, but because Pitt contemplated a vast sphere of British influence in the Americas. No more would Britain be humbled and Spain ascendant. John Meares had returned to England and described what happened at Nootka in inflammatory and not particularly accurate language. Press reports were even more provocative. At Nootka, Britain exulted, Spain had walked into a trap. By seizing British ships on dubious grounds, Martinez had given Pitt an excuse to declare war on Spain.

With a figurative slap of the national duelling glove, Britain prepared a memorial demanding satisfaction for the insult suffered at Nootka. Spain must admit it had no sovereignty whatever over Nootka or the Northwest Coast. And it must declare it would take no further actions against British subjects on the coast.

To back up their demands, the British recruited, often forcibly, hundreds of men to serve aboard its warships and sent the Spanish ambassador a note saying Britain intended to defend its subjects on the coast. In a spurt of patriotic fervour, members of Parliament—whom Thomas Jefferson termed "insolent bullies"—agitated either for war or for the payment of enormous damages. The leader of the Opposition in Parliament was even more adamant. "We now have the opportunity," he declared, "and ought to embrace it, of putting an end to the assertion of [Spain's rights in the Americas] forever." Long a virtually unknown shore on the opposite side of the world, the Northwest Coast and what became known as the Nootka Crisis had emerged as the flashpoint of a European confrontation.

The Dutch fleet joined the British. Warships put to sea. Spain's proposal for mutual disarmament was rejected.

The lobbying and jockeying for position went on, and the rhetoric escalated. Spain was far from silent: memoranda setting out Spain's position went to every major European capital. But Spain was without its most powerful ally. From 1789 on, France was consumed by revolution and the monarchy was all but destroyed. Carlos IV of Spain could expect little help from his embattled cousin Louis XVI.

As the dispute between Spain and England burgeoned, Spain had at least been able to stop worrying about Russian activity on the coast. Spain had protested to the Tsarina Catherine about Russian plans for Nootka and the Northwest Coast. Catherine replied that, in fact, the men in charge at Kamchatka had already been ordered not to move into any area claimed by another nation. If they had disobeyed this order, then all could be amicably resolved. The Russian expedition that was to sail south to Nootka was cancelled.

Britain, however, had no intention of backing down and refused to accept Spain's suggestion of arbitration by a neutral third party. As August 1790 drew to a close, war seemed imminent. Then, rather than risk all-out war in Europe, Spain wisely decided to mitigate its claims to this far-off and not particularly significant region. At the end of October, Britain and Spain signed the first Nootka Convention. It set out that buildings and land occupied by British subjects at Nootka in 1789 and wrested away by Martinez should be restored to those British subjects. Spain would make reparation for any seizure of ships and dispossessions. Neither nation would prevent the other from navigating, settling, trading, or fishing in the region. Britain would undertake to keep its subjects from trading with Spanish settlements.

Delicately couched and ambiguously worded so that both sides could save face, the agreement invited argument. Did the two countries agree that Britain had these rights only north of Nootka? Spain thought so. Britain claimed rights anywhere north of San Francisco Bay—and there were other points of contention. War had been avoided, but further disagreement was inevitable.

8

Eliza Heads North

IN THE MONTHS BEFORE THE signing of the Nootka Convention, the king, his ministers, and Revillagigedo and Bodega agreed that Spain must maintain her position on the Northwest Coast. To bolster that position, Bodega, under the viceroy's orders, sent ships north once more in early 1790. On April 1, after a stormy trip, the frigate *Concepción* and the supply ship *San Carlos* arrived off Nootka. The frigates *Princesa* and *Aranzazu* were to follow shortly after. They could not immediately enter Friendly Cove. Gales roared in from the Northeast, driving the ships away from shore, and wind and waves swept two crew members to their deaths. It took four days for the winds to abate and for the ships to make their way into the cove.

Eliza Heads North

Bodega had written in his instructions to expedition commander Francisco de Eliza that, although Spain had undoubted claim to the region, the king wished to establish "perfectly friendly harmony and good relations" with the British. Therefore, the events of the previous summer must not be repeated and Eliza should show courtesy to any foreign ships that might arrive. Nonetheless, if any showed disrespect to the Spanish flag, then he must use force to avenge the insult. Eliza must have breathed a sigh of relief to discover on arrival that no American, English, or Russian ship lay at anchor there. His tasks would be difficult enough without immediately walking that tightrope.

Foreshadowing what would be agreed on later that year in the Nootka Convention, he was instructed to give back to the English anything they could prove belonged to them in and around Nootka. Perhaps, wrote Bodega, it would be possible to avoid hostilities by finding a new location for a base on Juan de Fuca Strait, where the Spanish could be unmolested but aware of any ships that sailed the region.

Eliza was also to work on the survey of both the strait and the neighbouring coast so that a line could be drawn on the map dividing lands that belonged to Spain alone and those that could be shared between Spain and Britain. He should co-operate in any such survey with two English ships said to be on their way. He should also report on various aspects of the area and its people, and trade the copper sheets in his hold for sea otter furs.

And he must do all this even though two of the men under his command were carrying substantial grievances. The viceroy had instructed Bodega to name Martinez as second-in-command of the expedition, but Bodega had been dubious, since his mere presence would be enough to infuriate both British traders and the Nuu-chah-nulth, who would not easily forget the manner of Callicum's death. Instead, he placed Martinez in charge of trading for sea otter furs. Told the news, Martinez was bitter: he felt he had done his best in a difficult situation. He asked that he be transferred back to Spain. No response arrived before the expedition left, and he sailed with it to Nootka. When permission for the transfer finally arrived at Nootka in July, he left for San Blas, and, eventually, Spain.

Although Eliza had been ordered to find a replacement post for Nootka, he still needed to confirm Spain's claim to Friendly Cove. To aid him in this task, Revillagigedo had assigned the First Company of Catalonian Volunteers, a military unit that had fought in various revolts and rebellions in Mexico. Their commander, Pedro de Alberni, had remonstrated vigorously when he was informed of the new posting. Their weapons were old and almost useless, he declared; he needed more men and more warm clothing for all. Also, the soldiers had not been paid for two months and must receive their wages before departing. The argument with Antonio Villa Urrutia, in charge at Guadalajara, grew more heated. Villa Urrutia ordered Alberni to consider himself under arrest. The viceroy backed Villa Urrutia, saying Alberni should remain under arrest until the ships reached Nootka. Bad feelings were the inevitable result.

Alberni, however, was too professional to shirk his task of preparing for the defence of Nootka. Sailors and soldiers emplaced cannons on the land and dug trenches for defensive positions. Alberni assigned eleven men to the *Concepción* to ward off attack from the sea. Fifteen Volunteers on land watched over the ship and guarded the outside of the fortification. A further eleven stayed inside the new fort as a last line of defence.

The soldiers also planted a garden, seeding vegetables each week to determine the best planting times. Barley, potatoes, and beans did best, they found, with cabbages, garlic, spinach, beets, and other root vegetables also doing well. Chickens, cows, pigs, turkeys, and sheep added to the Spaniards' diet—and to the diet of the rats that had come off the various ships, who consumed both vegetables and baby chicks.

With the settlement well under construction, Eliza dispatched two expeditions from Nootka. Though Russia had pledged not to move into Spanish territory, Spain still needed to consolidate her claims to the northern portion of the coast. Sailing north toward Alaska, Salvador Fidalgo, on board the *San Carlos*, took possession of Cordova Bay in Prince William Sound and named another location Valdez Bay; both names remain on today's map. At three locations along the coast, he repeated the formal ceremonies of possession performed in 1779 and 1788. He performed yet another such ceremony just south of three Russian posts. Though a Russian agent sought a meeting, Fidalgo instead continued on until he turned back south in mid-August. He had hoped to return, as commanded, to Nootka, where he could share the results of his voyage, but the winds drove him west and south, and he headed instead for Monterey and then San Blas.

The second expedition was sent south from Nootka, both to seek a new location for a Spanish post and to investigate, as always, the possibility of a northwest passage. At the end of May the *Princesa Real,* which had followed the two other ships to Nootka, sailed out of Nootka Sound with Manuel Quimper commanding and Haro as pilot. They went ashore in Clayoquot Sound. There they discovered that Maquinna, on finding out that Martinez had returned to Friendly Cove, had retreated to the village of Wickanninish, another powerful chief. Quimper reassured him that Eliza, not Martinez, was in charge of the Spanish and that Martinez had a much reduced role. Somewhat hesitant and suspicious, Maquinna nonetheless said he would return to Friendly Cove.

The *Princesa Real* continued south, with the crew charting harbours that might serve as a Spanish base. Quimper explored the south shore of Juan de Fuca Strait, though he was unable to untangle the waterways that would have led him into Puget Sound. He did find Haro Strait and considered following it north, but, expected back at Nootka by mid-August, decided to stay within Juan de Fuca Strait. On the south shore near the entrance to the strait, they found a bay that looked like it might answer the Spaniards' need for a harbour to replace Friendly Cove. They named it Boca de Nuñez Gaona, for a Spanish naval commodore.

The crew traded with the Makah near here, gathering sea otter pelts in return for copper sheets. The Spaniards also bartered for giant salmon and berries to supplement their monotonous diet. But they soon learned that the Makah would defend their territory against any incursions when they attacked a crew member who had wandered away from the shore party in search of salmonberries. Nonetheless, they took possession of the area with the usual pomp and ceremony.

They then headed back toward Nootka, but, like Fidalgo before them, were forestalled. For six days, the lookouts peered fruitlessly into heavy fog, the ship tossed by currents that carried them away from Vancouver Island. Finally, his supplies diminishing and no change of weather in sight, Quimper, too, headed south for Monterey, carrying in the hold more than two hundred sea otter pelts and having completed new charts of Juan de Fuca Strait.

Back at Nootka, Eliza had spent much time over the summer trying to mend the badly damaged relationship with the Nuu-chah-nulth. The death of Callicum still rankled, and many thought it must be avenged. One young warrior declared that he would kill Martinez. He and his companions launched an attack but were driven back by musket fire. The situation grew worse when some Spanish soldiers and sailors, needing planks for their settlement, tried to take some from the roofs of lodges in a nearby Nuu-chah-nulth village. Initially repulsed, they returned well-armed and drove the inhabitants away, taking the boards back with them. Deeply offended by the theft, Maquinna now wanted nothing to do with the Spanish.

Alberni decided to take a hand. Using the few words of the Nuu-chah-nulth language that he knew, he composed a song "celebrating the greatness of Maquinna" and the friendship Spain felt for Maquinna and his nation. Maquinna was somewhat won over, but continued asking when the Spanish would leave, since he wanted his village site back.

Relations further improved when Martinez departed. But Eliza now had another problem: the irascible Colnett was back, hoping to reclaim his ship, the renamed *Princesa Real*. He also had every intention of breaking his pledge not to trade on the coast, considering it was extracted under duress. Once he arrived off the coast, Colnett dispatched his longboat to trade as far north as Clayoquot Sound, where he would meet up with it. At Clayoquot, Colnett bartered for all the furs that he could obtain. Not sure what might await him at Friendly Cove, he sent Hudson out in a small boat to go to Nootka to find out if his *Princess* was there. It was a foolish move: by now it was mid-October, the season of storms and treacherous waves. The small boat was smashed onto the rocks, and Hudson and all his men drowned. Knowing nothing of the calamity, Colnett sent the longboat out to reconnoitre. It returned from Nootka in mid-December with the news that the Spanish were at Nootka but that the *Princess Royal* was not. Colnett had treated Wickanninish and the Nuu-chah-nulth at Clayoquot badly; fearing their revenge, he decided he would winter at Nootka.

When he arrived, he found near disaster. The Spaniards were suffering from a host of ailments, including scurvy, dysentery, rheumatism, and flatulent colic; the sights and sounds inside their rudimentary dwellings can only be imagined. Rain, cold, and rats had destroyed much of the Spaniards' provisions. The *Princesa Real* and the *San Carlos* had not reappeared to unload what remained of their supplies to sustain the settlement over the winter. The Nuu-chah-nulth had their own problems, and all Eliza's urging could not persuade them to bring salmon and other provisions.

They had hoped to establish herds of domestic animals at Nootka; now they must slaughter their stock or starve. But what they had, they shared. Colnett and his officers were welcome to dine aboard the Spanish ships, and Eliza even gave him some of the last remaining prized hogs and chickens. In return, Colnett gave Eliza sugar and wine.

Not that this cordiality changed Colnett's mind or his intentions. He wanted his ships back and was disgusted that the *Princess Royal* was by now en route to Hawaii. He still traded for every sea otter fur he could get his hands on, in direct disregard of his promises to Bodega. He still blustered and employed braggadocio in speech and writings. By the time he finally regained his ships in 1791, Spain could only be glad that he would trouble them no more.

9

The Thinking Man's Voyage

THE NEW YEAR BROUGHT NO better weather. Three men had died in November and December, and by March, 32 of the 250 Spaniards at Nootka were in the shore hospital, so crowding it that Eliza had to build a shelter on the *Princesa* to house the sick. Colnett sailed away at the beginning of March still complaining, despite the hospitality he had received. Not long after, the *Princesa* sailed for San Blas with the sick men on board, in the hopes that returning them to a better climate would cure them. At the end of March, the *San Carlos*, under Ramón Saavedra, arrived with new supplies and new orders. Eliza was instructed to explore and chart from Mount St. Elias, at the head of the Alaska Panhandle, through Bucareli Bay, north of the Queen Charlotte Islands. He should then continue south, seeking any openings that might penetrate deep into the continent and might be the long-sought-after northwest passage. Then he should chart Clayoquot Sound and Juan de Fuca Strait before continuing to Alta California.

The instructions were fuelled by Spain's changing ambitions. Viceroy Revillagigedo was intent upon shoring up his nation's position on the Pacific coast from South America to Alaska. He agreed with Bodega that this could best be done by giving up Nootka and establishing a new base on Juan de Fuca Strait. All of Spain's efforts could then go toward what the foreign ministry in Madrid had told him was most important: drawing a line from the entrance of the strait north to latitude 60° north and enforcing the claim that everything east of that line lay within Spain's dominions. To do this, Spain would need to know more about the coast.

Bodega had told Eliza to take the warship *Concepción* exploring, but Eliza had a better idea: leave the *Concepción* to guard Nootka, where her size and armament could intimidate any foreign visitors, and sail the *San Carlos* along the coast. Smaller than the *Concepción*, the *San Carlos* could more easily be manoeuvred into narrow channels.

A second ship, captained by José Maria Narváez, would accompany the *San Carlos*. John Meares might not have recognized the ship he built in 1788 as the *Northwest America*. The schooner, confiscated, rebuilt, and renamed the *Santa Gertrudis la Magna* by Martinez in 1789, had been rebuilt once more in 1790 and renamed the *Santa Saturnina*.

The Thinking Man's Voyage

Before they left, the sailors petitioned Our Lady of the Most Holy Rosario, the patron saint of Spanish sailors, for a safe voyage. The men carried her image ashore to an altar and said a mass, asking for the Virgin's kindness on their voyage. The following day, blessed by God and impelled by Spain's ambitions, the ships set out.

They reached Cape St. Elias at the western end of Kayak Island, but did not do much charting. Instead, perhaps following secret orders, Eliza returned to the west coast of Vancouver Island, and the two ships explored Clayoquot and Barkley Sounds. The *San Carlos* then anchored off the southern tip of Vancouver Island, and the *Saturnina* joined her soon after. Crew manned the smaller boats and explored along the shore. On July 31, Eliza sent out the *Saturnina*'s longboat, under José Verdía, to chart Haro Strait.

That night, Verdía hastened back under cover of darkness. He reported that he had been surrounded by six canoes of Native people intent on attack. He fired on them, escaped, was surrounded again, fired again, and killed some of the Natives. Then the canoes moved in on the *Saturnina*. Eliza ordered the guns fired, and the attackers were deterred. Nervous but determined, the Spanish sailed on into the expanse of Juan de Fuca Strait, and continuing on between islands and through Active Pass, entered a broad expanse of water that they named the Gran Canal de Nuestra Señora del Rosario la Marinera, thus commemorating their patron saint. A year later, George Vancouver would cast off the religious imagery in favour of the secular and rename the waterway the Gulf of Georgia, in honour of King George III.

Their path now took them across the Juan de Fuca Strait. Narváez and the *Saturnina* sailed into Boca de Bodega (Boundary Bay), past Point Roberts, and through "a line of water that was more sweet than salty." They concluded this must flow from a large river, but could not see the entrance to the Fraser River. With information from the Musqueam that the canal continued much farther north, the two ships separately criss-crossed from eastern to western shore, mapping islands and sounds along the way as far as present-day Comox. Then, time and supplies exhausted, they rendezvoused on the south shore of Juan de Fuca Strait.

The waters that lead into Puget Sound beckoned, but circumstances dictated a different course. Even though one of the men had shot an elk that fed seventy men for three days, they were running short of fresh food, and sailors were showing the early symptoms of scurvy. Ever cautious and concerned about details, Eliza decided to transfer Narváez to the *San Carlos,* where the two men could collaborate on maps and journals and take both ships home to Nootka. It was now almost the end of July, and the *San Carlos* took almost three weeks to arrive at Nootka. Unsuited to such sailing, the *Saturnina* was still making little headway after two weeks. Running low on fresh water, the new captain, Juan Carrasco, was forced to turn south for Monterey and San Blas.

The Thinking Man's Voyage

Partly because of Eliza's caution, partly because of circumstance, the year's exploration was over and the officers and pilots spent the next weeks recording all they had seen and discovered.

* * *

Through the last half of the seventeenth and into the eighteenth century, a new movement gathered momentum in Europe. Out with superstition and tradition, its proponents chorused, and in with reason and reform. The major thinkers of this Age of Enlightenment promoted the use of the scientific method and encouraged intellectual discovery.

The Bourbon kings of Spain, in particular Charles III, who ruled from 1759 to 1788, saw such thinking as the way to reform a moribund Spanish bureaucracy and bring Spain back to glory. The king was ably aided by his chief minister, José Moñino y Redondo, the Count of Floridablanca. Charles IV, who succeeded Charles III, was not nearly as effective—or as interested—in affairs of state. Despite court intrigues, Floridablanca managed to keep his position and his influence as a backer of science and reason until 1792, when he was ousted and imprisoned. Under his sponsorship, Spain's scientists and geographers were able to keep moving forward.

Together with a healthy interest in the money to be gained from trade in the far reaches of the world, the ideas of the Enlightenment underlay the great voyages of the late eighteenth century. British navy officer James Cook made his three major voyages of discovery under the sponsorship of The Royal Society of London for Improving Natural Knowledge (more commonly known as The Royal Society). The French explorer Lapérouse set out in 1785 to sail around the world, carrying with him many scientists whose aim was not just to complete maps of the areas they passed through but also to enhance scientific knowledge and expand French prestige. Like Cook before him, Lapérouse sailed along the Northwest Coast.

Cook and Lapérouse published accounts of their journeys in the Pacific. Spain now realized that its policy of keeping its own discoveries secret was not such a good idea: if no one knew about the journeys, how could Spain be regarded as a first-class exploring nation, and how could Spain's claims to possession of the Northwest Coast be sustained?

To feature its own scientific and ethnographic discoveries, the Spanish government conceived of a wide-ranging expedition, with scientists and navigators aboard, that would bring home new discoveries, fill in the map of the uncharted world, and record much information on the residents, botany, zoology, and resources of each region they visited.

Commander Alejandro Malaspina, who had sailed around the world in 1786–88 seeking new trade opportunities for Spain, was selected to lead the expedition, with

José Bustamente y Guerra as co-leader. With them would go noted naturalists, pilots, surgeons, astronomers, geographers, and artists. Two corvettes, the *Descubierta* and the *Atrevida*, named to honour Captain Cook's ships the *Discovery* and the *Resolution*, were carefully designed to meet the demands of the expedition and built in Spain. Sixteen officers and eighty-six young men, carefully selected for "strength, intelligence and moral reputation," crewed each ship.

The expedition set out from Cadiz in 1789. They rounded Cape Horn and weighed anchor at Valparaiso, Callao, and Acapulco, whence Malaspina went overland to Mexico City. While he was there, new orders from the king arrived. A reputable French geographer had declared he thought it highly likely that Lorenzo Ferrer Maldonado had been telling the truth when he wrote his colourful tale about traversing the "Straits of Anián" from Atlantic to Pacific in 1588. Instead of the planned voyage to Hawaii and Kamchatka and on to Alaska, the Spaniards were to test this theory by setting out more directly for the Northwest Coast. They loaded aboard enough bread and salt pork for close to a year, vinegar and olive oil sufficient for two years, dried vegetables enough for seven or eight months, and a good deal of wine, enough for eighteen months to two years. Notwithstanding the loss by desertion of more than ninety men, the ships were more or less fully staffed when they left Mexico.

Malaspina and Bustamente were determined to avoid some of the dangers that faced ships' crews on such voyages. Tomás de Suría was a draftsman aboard the *Descubierta*; his journals are the only unofficial record of the voyage. "Our commander," Suría wrote, "has ordered the sailors to clean ship three times, making them take out their clothing and the rest of their luggage from between decks . . . in order to ventilate it." The doctor used a eudiometer to measure the sweetness or foulness of the air in various parts of the ship and declared it generally good.

Suría wrote eloquently of conditions aboard ship. He had no wish to complain, he said, just to record. "Stretched in my bed my feet were against the side of the ship and my head against the bulkhead . . . From my breast to the deck which was my roof, the distance is only three inches. This confined position does not allow me to move in my bed and I am forced to make for myself a roll of cloth to cover my head, although this suffocates me, but this is a lesser evil than being attacked by thousands of cockroaches, which are such a great pest that you see some individuals with sores on their foreheads and bites on their fingers." This was a shared officers' cabin; what conditions were like for the ordinary members of the crew, Suría does not say.

If the Straits of Anián truly existed, they should be found in the vicinity of latitude 60° north. On June 23, the ships' crews sighted their first land on the north coast; on the 24th, they reached 58° north. The next day, they approached Cape Fairweather and viewed the stupendous mountains beyond. On June 27, they drew into Yakutat Bay in Alaska. In this vicinity, the geographer on board sighted an opening that seemed to lead through the mountains.

"Great was the joy of the commander and of all the officers," recorded Suría, "because they believed and with some foundation, that this might be the much desired and sought-for strait . . . for the discovery of which a great reward has been offered."

Malaspina had with him Maldonado's account, and the officers now scrutinized both it and the landscape. "Even the figures and the perspective agree with what he gives," exulted Suría. "Transported with joy our commander steered toward the opening," but as the waters shallowed, Malaspina decided to anchor in nearby Port Mulgrave.

First, though, he needed to deal with two canoes of First Nations people that drew alongside. The Natives chanted and sang, following along as the ships bore for Port Mulgrave; some came aboard to trade sea otter skins. Once anchored, Malaspina prepared to dispatch the ships' boats to explore for the passage while going ashore himself to supervise the setting up of an astronomer's tent, and talking and trading with the Natives.

Three days later, wood and water gathered and the boats prepared, they headed out with supplies for fifteen days to seek the fabled straits. Though they soon suspected that the inlet led nowhere, they at first refused to give up. But the

Alejandro Malaspina's ships anchored at Port Mulgrave, at the north end of the Alaska Panhandle on Yakutat Bay, where the officers and crew met with a First Nation—probably Tlingit—of the region. There, they viewed what they termed the pyres and sepulchres of the chief (*cacique*), An-Mau. UBC LIBRARY RARE BOOKS AND SPECIAL COLLECTIONS

glaciers calved, and ice was all around them. There was no passage. Wrote Malaspina on a paper that they then put into a bottle and buried under a stone: "In the year 1791 the long-boats of his Majesty's *Descubierta* and *Atrevida* discovered this port which they named 'Disengaño' [Disappointment]."

One sailor was not quite ready to abandon the search. As the boats prepared to leave the bay, the crew realized that Able Seaman Manuel Fernandez was missing. Veering between annoyance that the man had disappeared and fear that he was lying injured somewhere or had been eaten by bears, the men sought him. At last, after shouts and gunshots had gone unanswered, the man reappeared. He had overheard the officers saying they had not surveyed the end of one of the inlets. Wanting to gain glory, he had set out overland, over rocks and ice "of a ruggedness truly difficult to imagine," to check out the inlet by land. When he finally returned, he confirmed the bad news: there was no passage inland.

Was there any point in continuing to explore the region? Malaspina decided not. Disappointed but not particularly surprised, he had never put much faith in the Maldonado account, referring to efforts to prove it as "futile." But it had to be done, if only to disprove the facile pronouncements of geographers who had never visited the region.

The ships turned south for Nootka, battling wind and waves for most of their voyage and often at a loss for a safe anchorage at which to ride out the weather. Just off the Queen Charlotte Islands at the beginning of August, whales and porpoises surfaced and sounded in great numbers, a sign, the mariners had learned, of an imminent change in the weather. The wind strengthened from the southeast until, on the night of August 5, "the wind could more justly be called a fully developed hurricane."

The wind was so strong, Suría noted, that they had to furl most of the sails, keeping only the topsail and the fore-sail unfurled. Rain swept down in torrents. "The rolls were tremendous and the darkness terrifying." They ran before the wind for six days, says Suría, though Malaspina suggests a shorter duration:

There was not a man who could keep his footing, simply from the violence of the wind, so that besides the mountains of water and foam which swept over us, there arose from the surface of the water small drops of spray forming a strange and copious rainfall never before seen. The roaring noise of both elements was horrible and terrifying. The confusion and shouting on the ship, together with the maledictions of the sailors, who in such cases break out into blasphemy, augmented the terror to such an extent that it seemed as if all the machinery of the universe were ready to destroy us. During this time we suffered such inconveniences as cannot be described, for during the six days there was no one who could get repose for a moment.

To thank the men for their efforts and to keep at bay the symptoms of scurvy that had begun to appear, Malaspina broke out the lemon syrup. On August 12, they arrived at Nootka. They found a settlement much happier than it had been over the winter. Malaspina described the wooden plank huts that housed the men and the various functions of the camp, "the bakery, which daily supplied fresh bread to all, the vegetable gardens, in which nature was already providing generously; the protection of the stores and equipment against a highly destructive swarm of rats; the forges; the preservation of additions to the dwellings."

Malaspina and his men set up an observatory onshore for astronomical observations and began charting the harbour and its surroundings, sending the launches off for a week-long surveying trip. In the meantime, they cut firewood, replaced damaged spars, made a new topmast, repaired sails, and brewed spruce beer, both for their use aboard the ships and to show those at Nootka how to make it as a specific against scurvy. They also lent their forges, blacksmiths, and armourer to help out the settlement, and gave those at Nootka anything they did not absolutely need for the voyage back to Mexico: cloth, wax, pea jackets, instruments for the sick bay, bouillon tablets, flour, medicines, wine, and whatever other supplies they could spare.

They sent out invitations to the Native groups of the area, hoping they could find out about their "customs, dress, physiognomy" and all the other parts of their lives. They also tried to trade for sea otter skins, but soon discovered that the First Nations possessed few, since they had traded most pelts to Colnett the previous year. What they had, they would not part with cheaply: they scorned beads and some pieces of cloth, some accepting only glass windowpanes, firearms, and blue cloth, while others chose gunpowder, sails, and hemp ropes.

Under Eliza, relations between the Nuu-chah-nulth and the Spaniards had been strained, partly because of the actions of Martinez, which would not be soon forgotten, partly because Colnett and his men had tried to poison them against the Spanish, and partly because the Nuu-chah-nulth chiefs wanted no permanent non-Native settlement in their territories. Even Alberni's song for Maquinna had not completely repaired the breach. Malaspina was very diplomatic; he also had more gifts to give and trade goods to barter with. Nuu-chah-nulth fishermen came daily to barter fish, and Maquinna, among others, sold the officers some of the young slaves they had, "either for two muskets or for one or two sheets of copper." This trade seemed satisfactory on both sides, the Nuu-chah-nulth obtaining needed goods in exchange for their prisoners, and the Spaniards taking various children to San Blas, where, living with the families of sailors, they might become good Catholics, learn Spanish, and serve as translators on later voyages.

When the Nuu-chah-nulth paddled a great canoe into the harbour, Malaspina and his officers were enchanted. "Some thirty men [were aboard]," wrote Suría, "whose chants, manoeuvres and skill surprised us in their first turns around the corvettes." Then the paddlers performed dances and sang, both on board the ships and on shore. Suría sketched all these activities. Two brothers came aboard and described Nuu-chah-nulth life and customs. "They gave us information so clear and strange about their religion, origins, laws, customs and system of government, commerce and inland geography that we could hardly believe that we were understanding each other so quickly and that the door had been so easily opened to mysteries of the greatest importance," wrote Malaspina.

Maquinna made a final plea to his new friends. Because the Spanish had appropriated his village site and therefore cut him off from the bounty of the sea, he was unable to feed himself and his family, and he was weak and emaciated. He would be happy to see the Spanish move from this site so he could reclaim his traditional land. Despite his unhappiness, he nonetheless confirmed, or so Malaspina said, that he had indeed ceded to the Spanish the land for the Nootka settlement, a matter of great importance in the negotiations that would take place the following year.

Their missions accomplished, Malaspina, Bustamente, and the two ships set sail from Nootka at the end of August, headed south for Monterey and carrying with them the maps and journals of a great voyage that would continue across the Pacific and back again to Spain. Sadly, though, politics would intervene: Malaspina would run afoul of internal schisms at the Spanish court. Accused of conspiring against the state, he was sentenced to ten years' imprisonment. The voluminous documentation from his voyages was either confiscated and destroyed or hidden away by its authors, not to be revealed for many decades. Spain had missed its chance to be seen at the forefront of the intellectual revolution.

10

Strait Explorations

THE WARSHIP *SANTA GERTRUDIS* DREW into Friendly Cove in late April 1792. Not long after, the Spanish ships *Activa* and *Aranzazu* anchored in the cove. Before the end of fall, five other Spanish ships would sail the Northwest Coast. That same spring, summer, and fall, thirteen British ships, five Americans, four under Portuguese registry, and, for good measure, one under French and one under Swedish registry, would arrive, some leaving Nootka fairly quickly, some staying longer. The year 1792 would represent the apex of European exploration and trading in the region, activity not to be repeated until well into the nineteenth century.

The heavy Spanish presence in the region was no coincidence. Facing Britain's challenge to her territorial claims,

Madrid wanted to show as strong a hand as possible in any negotiations. Spain needed to reaffirm its claims by once more trying to map those parts of the coast still uncharted. It must either verify or put to rest once and for all the possibility of a northwest passage. And it must send an envoy to Nootka to fulfill, with a British envoy, the terms of the Nootka Convention signed in 1790.

Viceroy Revillagigedo thought these purposes could best be accomplished through a major voyage, the Expedition of the Limits, which would chart Juan de Fuca Strait, go to Nootka to negotiate with a British envoy, and head north to map the coast. Building on explorations the previous year, Spain could abandon Nootka and replace it with a new post on Juan de Fuca Strait, "Spain's last possession on the northern coasts of California." Freed from the expense and confrontations inevitable at Nootka, Spain could proceed to draw its line north from the entrance to Juan de Fuca Strait, the waters and lands east of which would be the country's unchallenged preserve.

As ever, communication between the New World and the Old was sporadic, and Revillagigedo received no new instructions for action on the Northwest Coast. Unbeknownst to the viceroy, Madrid was once more in turmoil. The king's chief minister, the Count of Floridablanca, had been deposed in a palace coup and thrown into prison. Left to his own judgement, the viceroy directed Bodega, now in charge at San Blas, to mount the massive Expedition of the Limits.

Bodega himself was to lead the expedition and act as Spain's envoy in negotiations with the British.

Bodega was not so sure. Knowing the coast and its difficulties as well as he did, he doubted that a single expedition could accomplish all these aims in a single summer. He and the viceroy agreed, therefore, that a second expedition would take on the task of exploring Juan de Fuca Strait and its arms and inlets. Who would lead this expedition? The viceroy and the commandant had an easy choice close at hand: our old friend and experienced coastal hand, Francisco Mourelle, was the viceroy's secretary.

Still open in the naval archives were the journals of the men who had accompanied Martin de Aguilar along the coast in 1602. No one had found the "voluminous river" they reported at latitude 43° north. But mistakes in measuring latitude could easily be made, and the explorations of 1791 suggested that Juan de Fuca Strait and the arms that led from it might yet hold promise: perhaps the long-sought river might lie somewhere here. Mourelle was instructed to sail north to latitude 56° north in the schooner *Mexicana*, then explore southward to San Francisco, seeking particularly to determine once and for all whether any of the inlets or rivers that entered the sea led to Baffin or Hudson Bays.

Well aware how crucial good relations with the Native people would be to any Spanish claims, the viceroy directed that Mourelle should treat the Natives with humanity, gentleness, and gifts, "possibly pretending not to notice offences they commit." He should ensure that his men did not insult the Natives in any way, thereby "laying a foundation for a friendship perhaps very useful in the future to religion and the sovereign." Mourelle should not fire his guns unless he was fully prepared to justify such use when he returned to Mexico. He should, further, prepare the ground for fulfilling the Nootka Convention by finding a new harbour.

The *Mexicana* was to leave Acapulco by the end of 1791, accompanied by an armed longboat. But Alejandro Malaspina was at the Mexican port, and he was intrigued and excited by the possibility that somewhere off Juan de Fuca Strait lay a northwest passage. Why not, he suggested, send two ships—not with Mourelle, who, though undoubtedly competent, was not up to date on new techniques in astronomy and map-making, but with two of Malaspina's well-schooled officers. He prevailed: Mourelle fell conveniently ill, and Dionisio Alcalá Galiano was given command of the *Mexicana*. A second schooner, the *Sutil*, was rapidly built at San Blas, to sail under Cayetano Valdés.

As always, though, things weren't quite that simple. Built in a hurry and not particularly well, the *Mexicana* and *Sutil* needed a variety of modifications, including the raising of gunwales and decks. They finally left for Nootka in early March 1792, arriving two months later. The *Concepción* was still in port, the mainstay of the tiny settlement. Also on hand were the *Santa Gertrudis*, with Bodega on board, and a brig, *Activa*. (The *Santa Gertrudis* was a large warship sent from Spain to New Spain specifically to demonstrate Spain's naval might—not to be confused with the smaller *Santa Gertrudis la Magna*, now renamed the *Santa Saturnina*.)

Maquinna came out to welcome the new arrivals and to trade gifts and food with them. Second officer Secundino Salamanca wrote about the Nuu-chah-nulth in his journal, describing various ceremonies at length as well as their language, functions, and habits. He had ample time for this task: the *Mexicana* and the *Sutil* were once more in need of repair. They tried to leave for their explorations after three weeks but were stymied by contrary winds. Maquinna appealed to a Native god; whether that helped or not cannot be known, but the ships finally sailed out of Nootka on June 4.

Two days later, they arrived at Nuñez Gaona. There, they took aboard Tetacu, a local chief who wanted a lift home to Esquimalt and who promised to help guide them. They proceeded along the north shore of the strait, though the chief's wives were less confident and followed in canoes. At Esquimalt, Tetacu feted the Spaniards, told them there were other European ships in the vicinity, then waved them onward.

Using the information from the 1791 voyages, Galiano and Valdés continued their explorations through the San Juan Islands, charting and mapping as they went. They entered the Gulf of Georgia, then turned north and east, criss-crossing the Strait of Georgia, and greeting various

Native people who came out to meet their ships. On June 13, they met one of George Vancouver's ships, the *Chatham*. The respective officers made promises of mutual aid and did a little nationalistic posturing.

Captain George Vancouver had been appointed to represent Britain in discussions of how to implement the Nootka Convention. Instead of proceeding directly to Nootka, however, he had decided to explore and chart the Gulf of Georgia. By late June, the Spanish ships were anchored near Point Grey, off present-day Vancouver. As they breakfasted, the lookout spied a launch being rowed by Europeans. At first, Vancouver thought the *Sutil* and *Mexicana* were his own ships coming to find him, since he had been away from his ship *Discovery* for some time. The British sea captain and explorer was greatly disappointed. "I cannot avoid acknowledging that, on this occasion," he wrote, "I experienced no small degree of mortification in finding the external shores of the gulf had been visited, and already examined a few miles beyond where my researches during the excursion had extended."

Swallowing his chagrin at not being first, he complimented the Spanish, for their conduct "was replete with that politeness and friendship which characterizes the Spanish nation; every kind of useful information they cheerfully communicated, and obligingly expressed much desire, that circumstances might so concur as to admit our respective labours being carried on together." Such mutual courtesy, one

Though these boats seen in Juan de Fuca Strait, followed by the canoes of First Nations people, are probably those of John Meares, sailing in 1786, the scene closely parallels that of Spanish explorers.
UBC LIBRARY RARE BOOKS AND SPECIAL COLLECTIONS

can't help thinking, might have come in handy when Martinez met Colnett; Galiano and Vancouver would probably not have brought Europe to the brink of war.

More or less together, for the larger, more seaworthy British ships were faster though less manoeuvrable, Vancouver and the Spaniards continued north, exploring each channel and bay they encountered and visiting back and forth. Galiano and Valdés, for example, travelled on board the *Discovery* with Vancouver for some distance up the gulf on June 24, telling Vancouver about Burrard Inlet and providing him with a copy of the map their artist had drawn.

They also exchanged information about a possible northwest passage. Vancouver reported in his journal that Natives on the coast had told Valdés the previous summer that the inlet described by de Fonte did indeed exist, and did communicate with a northern sea, but that Valdés put little credence in their story.

Naturalist Archibald Menzies noted that Galiano had come aboard the *Discovery* to suggest how the two groups might divvy up the surveying:

> the two parties to facilitate the examination of this intricate country, saying, that his Boats & Crews were ready to aid in the execution of any plan that might be devised for that purpose, & as his Vessels were of a small draught of Water they might be commodiously employed on difficult & distant excursions . . . & Capt Galeano then proposed to send one of his Boats to examine a large opening leading to the Northward & and on his returning on board, he dispatched Don Valdes Commander of the schooner upon that service.

All courtesies aside, Galiano was quite possibly intent that, as Spain's agent, he be the first to discover any northwest passage.

On north they went, each officer reporting to the others what they had charted and mapped. On July 13, the British and Spanish separated after exchanging copies of their surveys, the British to sail as rapidly as they could toward the north end of Vancouver Island and the channels that would

Dionisio Galiano and Cayetano Valdés sailed the Northwest Coast in 1792, spending time at Friendly Cove in Nootka Sound. This illustration, which appeared in the atlas published in 1802 that recorded their voyage, shows the Spanish flag flying over the cove, with the Spanish fortifications and Nuu-cha-nulth boats and houses, among other details. DAVID RUMSEY MAP COLLECTION, WWW.DAVIDRUMSEY.COM

take them around the tip of the island out into the open sea and south to Nootka. The Spanish chose to hug the mainland coast more closely. The small boats were rowed up each inlet, each declivity, that might lead somewhere east. Up Toba Inlet, up Knight Inlet, sketching and charting they went, sometimes paced by the Kwakwaka'wakw in their mighty canoes.

Though relations with the First Nations were generally good, some uneasiness persisted on both sides: the Natives wanted trade goods and arms the Spaniards were not willing to barter, and the Spaniards feared an attack. But only one small incident marred the general peacefulness, and that was swiftly resolved. The two ships spent some time anchored off Port Guemes (Port Hardy), then rounded the tip of Vancouver Island and sailed southeast back to Nootka, arriving on August 31.

George Vancouver had arrived at Nootka two days before Galiano and Valdés arrived. Bodega had been there since the spring. The stage was set for the last great confrontation between British and Spanish on the Northwest Coast.

CHAPTER

11

The Expedition
of the Limits

LATE IN 1791, JUAN FRANCISCO DE LA BODEGA Y QUADRA
bent over a synopsis of the diaries and charts compiled
through almost twenty years of Spanish exploration of the
Northwest Coast. Though he did not have on hand Cook's
diaries, he was aware of their general conclusions. And
he had his own knowledge of the coast, gleaned from his
adventuring back in 1775. From all this, he could formulate
instructions for the Expedition of the Limits and fulfill his
dual role as commander of the expedition and Spain's rep-
resentative in carrying out the Nootka Convention.

Bodega would go north on board the frigate *Santa
Gertrudis*. He would negotiate with the British representa-
tive the rights each country would have on the coast and

how much must be paid in reparations to John Meares. He would then turn Nootka over to the British commissioner and establish a new post on Juan de Fuca Strait. In addition, he would explore the coast north to latitude 56° north.

He could call on much support for his tasks. The frigate *Concepción* was still at Nootka, as it had been for two years now. The new brig *Activa*, and the frigate *Aranzazu* would follow Bodega north. The *Sutil* and the *Mexicana* would be in the vicinity.

Bodega arrived at Nootka in late April but found no sign of the British commissioner, George Vancouver. What he did find at Nootka was not encouraging. The previous winter had been as bad as the winter of 1790–91, cold and grey, with snow falling most of the winter and heavy rain the rest of the time. The men had again suffered from the usual ailments, and nine had died of them. Thirty-two others had been sent back to Monterey aboard the *Princesa*. The commandant's house, built of green wood, was in bad shape. If he were to receive the English in a manner befitting Spain's dignity and prestige, new houses must be built and agriculture re-established with the pigs, goats, sheep, and cows brought on board the ships.

Equally important, the ships must be repaired. The *Santa Gertrudis* had survived the pounding of the waves well, but the *Activa* was leaking and the *Aranzazu* needed to be careened and repaired. Galiano's ships drew into port, and they too needed substantial work done. While his men hammered and caulked, Bodega turned his attention to relations with the Nuu-chah-nulth.

Eliza had persuaded Maquinna that the Spaniards were to be trusted and could be good friends. Bodega wanted to go a step further, probably aware that a solid friendship with the Native chief would serve Spain's interests well when it came to negotiating with the British. Reassured, Maquinna moved back close to Bodega's quarters and often dropped by for dinner. "Upon hearing the dinner bell," wrote one of the Spaniards at the settlement, "Maquinna comes daily ... and sits at the Commander's side. He asks for anything he pleases." What pleased Maquinna were wine, sherry, coffee if there was any, and chocolate in the morning. Galiano's diary suggested that Maquinna used cutlery as well as the best-mannered European and amused "everyone with his festive humour." He usually brought his brother along and was often accompanied by other Nuu-chah-nulth. They were particularly fond of a type of black beans they termed "nobles' beans." Chief Tlu-pa-na-nootl also visited weekly, bringing venison with him, but he was judged not half as entertaining as Maquinna.

Maquinna's statements about Meares and company pleased Bodega. He had not, said the Nuu-chah-nulth chief, ceded land to Meares or his representatives but had simply allowed the Englishman to live there briefly; the only time he had ceded land was to the Spanish. Bodega wrote that, if only the Spaniards could stay here a little longer, they could civilize the Natives completely. Though he does not say so explicitly, he would certainly have wanted them to be converted to Catholicism, something the priests who had come to Nootka had scarcely attempted, blaming their failure on the lack of agricultural land that would have to underlie any missions here.

The botanist who accompanied Bodega, José Moziño, was most impressed by the Nuu-chah-nulth, objecting to the way they had often been portrayed as lower beings and petty thieves. It was the sailors, he proclaimed, who acted badly. "Either as a result of their almost brutal upbringing or because they envied the humane treatment the commandant and other officers always gave the Natives, [the sailors] insulted them at various times, crippled some and wounded others, and did not fail to kill several ... All the sciences and arts have no value if they serve only to make us cruel and haughty." The Nuu-chah-nulth, he said, were generally honest and gentle. "What a pity that they could not in general say the same about us."

The treatment accorded by the Spanish compared well with that meted out by American traders on the coast, who were more and more often using force instead of trade to get sea otter pelts. When some of the Nuu-chah-nulth brought to Nootka in early June a companion who had been shot, probably in an attack by American Robert Gray, Bodega had him treated by the settlement's surgeon and allowed him to recuperate at Nootka.

An artist on the Galiano/Valdés voyage drew this illustration of a Nootka celebration put on by Chief Maquinna to mark the entry of his daughter into puberty. DAVID RUMSEY MAP COLLECTION, WWW.DAVIDRUMSEY.COM

The *Aranzazu* arrived with more supplies on May 13. Bodega sent the *Concepción* back south with cargo intended for the California settlements and dispatched José Caamaño and the *Aranzazu* toward Bucareli Bay to undertake part of the Expedition of the Limits. Might the legendary strait supposedly sighted by Admiral de Fonte lie somewhere along this intricate coast that was yet to be properly charted? Caamaño was charged with finding out.

He performed the prescribed formal acts of possession on the Queen Charlotte Islands and at other stops he made along the coast. He honoured the now-deposed chief minister by naming a harbour near Dixon Entrance

Puerto Floridablanca. Crew members rowed the longboats up inlets and through narrow passageways, ever seeking, or seeking to disprove the existence of, a way to the east. The deep and vertiginous fjords that characterize the coast often beckoned but never delivered. Yet maps made by Colnett had seemed to indicate that a passage might yet exist.

Caamaño entered a large strait and sailed 160 kilometres north along it, hopeful and skeptical by turns. Could this be the long-sought-after passage? They could not find out: bad weather forced them back. Finally, Caamaño turned south, with new charts but with the question he had been sent to answer still unresolved—though his own conclusion might be inferred from his decision to change the name of the waterway from Estrecho de Fonte (Straits of de Fonte) to Bocas y Brazos de Moñino (Entrance and Arms of Moñino). The following summer, Vancouver would sail through the again-renamed Clarence Strait and prove it was not the passage.

Had de Fonte's expedition been hope or hype? The tale had first appeared in the London publication *Monthly Miscellany or, Memoirs for the Curious* as an anonymous letter, probably penned by the mischievous editor of the periodical. Invented out of whole cloth, the yarn nonetheless had great appeal to those who wanted to believe in a northwest passage. It was taken up in 1744 by a critic of the Hudson's Bay Company to prod the British into a more energetic search. When two respected French geographers affirmed the story and mapped the supposed discovery, the hunt was on. Though Spanish critics had completely debunked the tale, their writings had not been published by the always secretive Spanish authorities.

Nootka was busy, but it was not the only Spanish settlement buzzing with life that hectic summer of 1792. Before he left San Blas, Bodega had instructed Salvador Fidalgo to take the *Princesa* back north to establish a new post on the south shore of Juan de Fuca Strait. By the time Galiano and Valdés had arrived at Neah Bay in early June, the settlement of Nuñez Gaona was taking shape in a wide clearing along the shore by the stream that tumbled into the ocean, with grass-thatched huts, a barracks with cannons mounted on top, and the required infirmary and oven. The men planted shoots that had already been started at San Blas so they could have fresh vegetables sooner and tended the sheep, goats, pigs, and cows they brought from there.

Would this settlement be the Spanish headquarters on the Northwest Coast? Fidalgo thought so, finding it beautiful, fertile, healthful, and in a great location, commanding the entry to the strait. Galiano and Valdés had weighed in on the negative. Nuñez Gaona might be everything Fidalgo said it was, but the cost of maintaining it would be high and efforts to sustain the settlement would be great. The two ships' captains had asked an increasingly obvious question: what advantages would any settlement so far from its centre of Spanish strength in Mexico confer?

The Expedition of the Limits

While Bodega was enjoying good relations with the Nuu-chah-nulth at Nootka, Fidalgo was having more difficulty. Though dealings between the two parties were generally friendly, Fidalgo and his men feared that the Makah, renowned in the region for their fierceness, might attack; they were also concerned about theft from the settlement or the ship. Because the surf and the rocky bottom offshore kept the *Princesa* out beyond a musket shot, a cannon was fired at dawn and dusk to warn off any Natives nearby. In case a quick retreat was needed, a longboat was kept on the shore so the men could depart rapidly for the safety of the *Princesa*.

Early in July, Fidalgo thought his worst fears had been confirmed. Returning to the *Princesa* after visiting a British trading ship, Fidalgo learned that his second-in-command, Antonio Serantes, had not returned from a visit ashore. Going ashore himself, he was told that Serantes had gone hunting with a Makah. Serantes did not return that night. The next morning, Fidalgo sent out a search party of twenty men accompanied by dogs. They found nothing. Then another Makah reported that Serantes had been killed by Makah chief Tutusi. Infuriated by the unsubstantiated report, Fidalgo ordered the cannon fired at two Makah canoes approaching the ship. All aboard one canoe, with the exception of a fifteen-year-old boy and a six-year-old girl, were killed. Several days later, Serantes's body was found.

As the news spread of the deaths, Tutusi asked for help from the Nuu-chah-nulth in taking revenge. Fidalgo wrote to Bodega detailing and justifying his actions, the letter carried to Nootka by a visiting ship's captain. Bodega was aghast. By a single thoughtless act, Fidalgo had put at risk all that Eliza and Bodega had established. He wrote back to Fidalgo, saying that Serantes's death was indeed horrific, but that Fidalgo had gone too far. "It does not seem right to me," he wrote, "that you should have taken vengeance on persons who might have been quite innocent and when the assassin is not known." Bodega further informed Revillagigedo of Fidalgo's actions; he in turn informed Madrid, and Fidalgo was chastised. Somehow, Bodega managed to smooth over relations with the Native groups. The summer wore on at Nuñez Gaona with no immediate decision on its future.

12

Two Empires Meet

FRANCIS DRAKE NEVER FORGOT THE day in 1568 when Spanish ships in the Caribbean trapped the English ships owned by his cousin. Though he escaped, Spain was his enemy from that day on, and he pirated and preyed at sea and on land throughout the Spanish realm in the Americas. The treasures he freebooted were his monetary reward; perhaps his greatest triumph for England was his sterling role in the English victory over the Spanish armada in 1588. His ghost was surely present at Nootka in 1792 as George Vancouver prepared to press Britain's claims to the Northwest Coast. For long before Bodega, thirteen years before the presumed voyage of Juan de Fuca, Drake had landed north of Spain's northernmost claims in Alta California, named the land

New Albion, taken possession for England, and founded a small settlement. Some say he left men behind as colonizers, but there is no real record of this.

George Vancouver undoubtedly thought of Drake as he finally coasted into Nootka on August 28, 1792. The official British envoy to Nootka, Vancouver had little doubt about his mission. According to the British interpretation of the first Nootka Convention, bolstered by the memory of Drake's claims, he would take over Nootka from the Spanish and consolidate Britain's claim to the coast from the Russian settlements in Alaska to just north of the Spanish missions at San Francisco. According to Britain, by signing the convention, Spain had acknowledged the claim and agreed to abide by it; the British map drawn in 1790 affirmed this position.

So certain was Vancouver that the turnover was just a formality that he kept Bodega waiting at Nootka while he fulfilled his other instructions to seek any possible northwest passage by examining all inlets and ascending all large rivers, and to check out any European settlements along the way. On his explorations, Vancouver investigated Puget Sound, the first of the explorers to do so, circumnavigated Vancouver Island and finally arrived at Nootka on August 28, prepared to take over.

He was in for a surprise. Bodega had used his four months of enforced delay wisely. When he arrived, he had been prepared to hand the area over to Britain. Floridablanca's letter for Bodega, delivered by Vancouver's store ship in midsummer, had instructed the Spaniard to restore to the British "the Buildings and Districts or parcels of Land which were occupied by [Britons] . . . in April 1789 as well as the port of Nootka . . . " But the more people he talked to over the summer, the less convinced he was of Britain's rights to anything at Nootka.

First into port was Francisco Viana, the Portuguese sailor who had acted as captain of John Meares's *Ifigenia Nubiana* in that fateful summer of 1789. Viana reiterated that the *Ifigenia* was under Portuguese registry, not British. But he wavered on the question of Meares's claim to land at Nootka. Meares, he said, had built only a very small house, and the Nuu-chah-nulth had torn it down as soon as Meares had left. Indeed, said Viana, Martinez was telling the truth when he said there was no evidence of a European settlement at Nootka when the Spanish captain arrived. Then Maquinna added in his story: won over by Bodega's charm and open-handedness, he declared that he had never sold Meares or any of his men any land at all. He had, however, allowed the Spanish to claim the land on the basis that if the Spanish left, it would revert to him.

As the summer wore on, others who had been at Nootka in 1789 returned. Americans Joseph Ingraham and Robert Gray arrived in late July. Ingraham told Bodega that Martinez had been helpful to the crew of the *Ifigenia* until he read in the ship's papers that any foreign seamen were to be apprehended; Martinez found this to be grounds for seizing the ship. But he did not act badly to the crews, said Ingraham, and he repaired the ship. The *Northwest America* was seized because its captain owed money to the Spanish. Ingraham confirmed that he had never heard that Meares had purchased any land from Maquinna.

Colnett, said Ingraham, had asserted that he was there to take possession for the British and had been informed that Spain had already been in possession for several years. These accounts and others convinced Bodega that Spain's rights superseded Britain's claims to Nootka.

When Vancouver finally arrived, he was welcomed with due pomp and ceremony, and Bodega offered the British officers every hospitality, with frequent banquets and gifts of supplies. Vancouver was invited ashore, where he set up an astronomical observatory and used some of the Spanish buildings. Vancouver's ships were careened, and repairs began. But Bodega also presented Vancouver with a letter outlining the events of 1789, together with the affidavits he had collected over the summer. Given these and the historical evidence that Spain had established a settlement here long before Britain ever thought of doing so, Spain was, he wrote, under no obligation to give up anything at all.

Bodega told Vancouver that he would, nonetheless, be willing to hand over Nootka, provided that Vancouver, for Britain, recognized Spain's claims to everything south of Juan de Fuca Strait and east of the line that was to be drawn north from the strait's entrance. Wined and dined

Vancouver was, but a patsy he was not. He declared that the Nootka Convention gave British subjects the right to access any point north of San Francisco. But, he said, he had no instructions to discuss anything other than the handover of Nootka, and no intention of doing so.

Bodega countered that the issue should be referred to their respective sovereigns for a decision. Meanwhile, he was willing to give up the precise area where Meares had established his small settlement. He would also put Nootka under Vancouver's command—but without prejudicing Spain's rights or claims to the region.

Vancouver was stymied. He intuited that the British Colonial Office wanted to establish a settlement on the coast, but he had no orders to do so himself. He didn't want to take over at Nootka unless Bodega recognized British rights to the region, but he did not want to leave Nootka unoccupied should the Spaniards depart, for who knows which nation might then move in? Russia was never far away, and American traders were always in the vicinity. Nootka was the best place for them to use as the headquarters for their fur trade.

At a stalemate, the diplomats took a break, rowing and sailing in small boats up the inlet to Maquinna's camp. The sailors beat the drums and played their fifes as they went, a response to the Nuu-chah-nulth practice of chanting and singing when they visited the Europeans. They pitched their tents not far from Maquinna's village, then pulled into the beach the following day, where, with great ceremony and decorum, both sides delivered speeches, presented gifts, and feasted. Maquinna's cooks had prepared porpoise, whale, seal, and other meats in boiling oil, but Vancouver and Bodega had brought what they considered a superior meal, with Bodega supplying the food and Vancouver the drink. Bodega even brought along the silver plate used on board his ship; the British commented that he must have had at least seventy settings of such plate, commonly used in Bodega's home city of Lima.

The Nuu-chah-nulth warriors danced and chanted; Maquinna's brother garbed himself in a helmet and coat of mail given to Maquinna by Bodega. Maquinna capped the dancing by suddenly jumping into the centre of the ring wearing a magnificent sea otter robe, a round black hat, and a traditional, impressive mask that could be changed by cords that the wearer pulled to reveal and hide a variety of faces. The warriors then gave the Europeans sea otter pelts. The Europeans did their best in return. To the music of the fifes, Vancouver's men performed a rustic dance and reel. The Europeans then returned to their tents and the next morning went back to Friendly Cove. Either now or several weeks hence, Bodega or Vancouver suggested that some part of the region be named after the two of them. And it was done: the large island mapped by both Spanish and British was labelled Quadra and Vancouver Island, though the "Quadra" was soon dispensed with on British maps.

It was an enchanting diversion, but it did nothing to unbolt the deadlock. Vancouver was convinced that the Americans had a hand in stiffening Bodega's resolve, but the provenance mattered not at all. Neither Bodega nor Vancouver would budge from their stated positions; neither would discuss any deviation from those positions

Now an incident with the Nuu-chah-nulth heightened the drama. A young cabin boy, a servant of Bodega, was found murdered in a particularly brutal manner. The Natives in the area immediately fled, fearing revenge. And revenge was indeed what the British and Americans had in mind. Ingraham arrested two of Maquinna's servants, who were taken with their arms tied to Bodega. Bodega refused to punish all for the acts of individuals. Asked to say who was guilty, Maquinna, deeply insulted at any insinuation that he might in some way be thought responsible, expressed his dismay that innocent people might be punished. "It would do me and my dignity an injustice to imagine that if I wanted to break the peace, I would order the assassination of a boy less able to defend himself than if he were a woman," he declared. "You would be the one whose life would be in greatest danger if we were enemies."

Maquinna, however, asked for Spanish assistance in punishing those who might possibly be responsible. Bodega refused to punish anyone whose guilt was unproven. At least one Englishman at Nootka was dismayed: hold Maquinna hostage until the guilty are delivered up, he advised. Bodega was too mild, too good; "he even treated the Indians more like companions than people who should be taught subjection." But Bodega prevailed, especially since it seemed the culprit might well have been a Mexican who had deserted from Bodega's own ship. Maquinna rewarded Bodega's restraint by executing a deed of gift for the land that Spain had settled.

The debate continued into September with no change in the participants' positions. Vancouver decided not to try to take Nootka by force. Madrid and London would have to decide the future of Nootka and the surrounding territory. With no solution forthcoming, Bodega decided he must leave, for he had been absent long enough from his work as commandant at San Blas. Vancouver and Bodega agreed that they would meet in Monterey before the end of the year. On his last night in the Northwest, Bodega and his officers went to a farewell dinner aboard the *Discovery*. The following morning, they exchanged thirteen-gun salutes, and the *Activa* sailed out of harbour, leaving Caamaño in charge. Seventeen years after he first sighted the Northwest Coast, Bodega said his last farewell to Nootka. By mid-October, Vancouver, too, had sailed south.

* * *

Bodega had one last task to perform in the Northwest. Bodega and Fidalgo had left San Blas before the viceroy received new instructions from Madrid about settlements on the coast. Nootka was not to be abandoned, said Revillagigedo in letters sent to both men, and no new post was to be established. Bodega may well not have received the instructions to abandon Nuñez Gaona, but, independently, he had decided this was the better course. He sent orders to Fidalgo to tear down what he had built.

After he left Nootka, Bodega sailed south to visit the tiny settlement. The captain of the *Activa* was not particularly familiar with the waters near Nuñez Gaona; becalmed, he anchored near Cape Flattery. Knowing the danger the ship was in, two American captains who were nearby sent out their longboats to tow it to safety. Were the Spaniards working furiously to free the ship from danger? No, discovered the Americans, totally bemused; they were celebrating mass. All dined aboard the *Activa* and, eventually, the ships arrived at Nuñez Gaona, where Bodega delivered his decision. Juan de Fuca Strait was a disappointment: no northwest passage opened from it into the continent. Fidalgo was ordered to take down all he had erected, bring it back to Nootka aboard the *Princesa*, and take over that settlement from Caamaño. Despite the continuing uneasy relations between the Spanish and the Makah, Bodega ordered that the barracks should be left for the Makah to use as they wished. On September 29, the Spaniards onshore retreated to their ships and sailed away from Neah Bay for the last time.

CHAPTER

13

The End of It All

WHEN BODEGA ARRIVED AT MONTEREY in early October 1792, orders from Madrid dated February 29 finally caught up with him. Fortunately, they approved Bodega's conduct with Vancouver: Spain did not agree to the cession of Nootka. Haro was dispatched post-haste to tell Fidalgo to keep those from nations other than Spain and Britain from trading in the area, unless they had specific permission from Spain to do so.

Haro arrived in late November. Ordered to remain, Salvador Fidalgo sought to make the best of yet another winter of misery, rain, and cold in Spain's last Northwest outpost. To hold the fort here, Fidalgo needed to improve Spanish defences. To keep his men busy, he set them to work improving the fortifications on San Miguel Island, erected in 1789, dismantled later that year and rebuilt by the Catalonian Volunteers in 1790.

By the end of winter, though, the Spanish were in no shape to defend their base. Rain had fallen incessantly for almost three months. The few vegetables they had been able to salvage rotted, their flour and bread were destroyed by the damp, and even their tobacco had run out. The Nuu-chah-nulth brought no fish or game from their winter village. Several of the men had died over the winter, and two-thirds of the *Princesa*'s crew were scurvy-ridden.

In mid-April, the British ship *Chatham*, captained by Peter Puget, returned to Nootka to continue Vancouver's charting of the coast. The British were able to supply the Spanish with flour, peas, and tobacco, which restored their spirits somewhat. The British stayed while their ship was repaired and recaulked, with Spanish carpenters helping the English and officers sharing meals onshore and on the ships. Though Maquinna had initially distrusted Fidalgo because of his conduct at Nuñez Gaona, he now softened his stance and moved back to his summer village north of the Spaniards, frequently bringing salmon and venison as gifts.

The *Chatham* left in mid-May; soon after, the *Discovery* hove into view. Vancouver spent a few days here, then continued on with his explorations. British and American traders came and went throughout the summer. Ramón Saavedra arrived aboard the *San Carlos* to take over Nootka;

Fidalgo gratefully departed aboard the *Princesa*. Saavedra mothballed the *San Carlos* for the winter of 1793–94 and moved to quarters on the land.

Bodega had spent a pleasant few months at Monterey, joined at the end of November by Vancouver and his men. Though he accepted that Nootka must be maintained as a matter of national honour until a final settlement could be reached with the British, Revillagigedo was weary of the continued expense associated with the Northwest Coast. It was useful to acquire sea otter pelts to trade for the mercury required for South American gold mining. But did the difficulty and expense warrant the result? He suggested to the officers of the *Sutil* and *Mexicana* that Spain had now attained as much nautical knowledge as would be useful. Some were aghast: the question of a northwest passage was not finally answered, and if Spain gave up the quest to British explorers, "[we] might well give them the glory, and we could not listen without covering ourselves with shame, if they should find the much desired passage to the other sea."

In the end, Revillagigedo ruled out more exploration of the Northwest Coast. "From now on a halt should be called to all projects obliging us to make great expenditures." He had neither the money nor the men to expel the Russians from their settlements. On arrival at San Blas, Fidalgo had reported that Vancouver's ships were heavily armed, and repeated rumours that the British might soon attack Monterey and San Diego. It would be difficult enough defending Spain's settlements on the California coast should the British choose to attack them. Give Nootka to the British, said Revillagigedo; let them deal with it. For the moment, though, he had to obey instructions from Madrid to protect Nootka until a final pact could be reached with Britain. In addition to the *San Carlos* at Nootka, in 1793 he sent the *Activa*, under Eliza, and the *Mexicana*, under Juan Martinez y Zayas, to explore south from Juan de Fuca Strait to San Francisco, ever seeking that elusive passage. Eliza, blaming adverse winds and a water shortage, accomplished little; he turned for home just half-way to Juan de Fuca. Martinez y Zayas waited for him for several months near Neah Bay, then turned south, too, even venturing a little way up the Columbia River but turning back because he ran aground and was made uneasy by the presence of large canoes of First Nations people. The dual expedition revealed no new site for a settlement near the strait, though the Spanish did establish a post at Puerto de la Bodega, sixty kilometres north of San Francisco.

As ever, events in Europe overtook events on the Northwest Coast. The execution of France's Louis XVI in January 1793 sent shivers down the spines of other European monarchs, especially the kings of Spain and Britain. When the new French government declared war against Britain and Spain soon after, the two combatants in the Northwest became allies in Europe. In no time at all, France, the United States, Britain, Spain, Holland, Austria, and Prussia were once more involved in manoeuvring and machinations in Europe and in North and South America. Temporarily allied, Britain and Spain signed the second Nootka Convention in February 1793, settling the claims of John Meares for much less than Meares claimed he was owed but much more than he probably deserved.

In April 1793, the Spanish court received Revillagigedo's recommendations. Neither Spain nor Britain had much real interest in Nootka; there were more important issues to consider. The British foreign office had its own recommendations. Britain should take over at Nootka while keeping the harbour open to both Spanish and British. Spain should yield its claims to lands immediately adjacent to Meares's claim. Talk about the fixing of boundaries or reservation of rights should cease. The foreign office recommended that the British flag be raised, and that both nations withdraw. Neither nation should erect any permanent structures—but both British and Spanish subjects would be free to put up temporary quarters.

The compromise was a retreat for Spain, but advancing claims in the Northwest or even maintaining the status quo no longer seemed very important while French troops were marching across the Pyrenees into Spain. On January 11, 1794, the two nations signed the third Nootka Convention "for the Mutual Abandonment of Nootka." The Nootka Crisis was over.

Meanwhile, another miserable winter was bedevilling the residents of Nootka. As in previous years, the

Nuu-chah-nulth under Maquinna had spent more time supplying sea otter pelts for trade than on storing up food for the winter. In addition, they were kept from their traditional fishing grounds by the presence of the Spanish. They were near starvation, helped only by Saavedra's supplying what food he could spare.

The *Aranzazu* arrived with supplies in early spring, then returned with additional provisions from Monterey. Revillagigedo had hoped that Bodega would return to Nootka to execute the terms of the third convention. But Bodega was a broken man, seriously ill and almost bankrupt. He wanted nothing more than to return to his birthplace in Peru and take up some less demanding post there. It was not to be: he died in Mexico City in March 1794.

José Manuel de Álava took over in his stead. Official instructions for the handover had still not arrived when he and Fidalgo left San Blas on board the *Princesa* in mid-June. Saying that news should be sent north as soon as it arrived, he would wait for such orders until October 15, then return to Monterey.

The *Princesa* arrived at Nootka at the end of August. Vancouver sailed into port the next day. Since neither had received definite orders, they could only wait while repairing the ships, visiting Maquinna and generally having a good time. Mid-October came without news, and they prepared to depart. Vancouver left first, with the Spanish flag still flying over Friendly Cove. Only when Fidalgo arrived back at Monterey did the orders at last arrive. A new British envoy had been sent to execute the convention's terms; Vancouver could now depart to complete his four-year round-the-world odyssey.

Machinations back in Spain continued, and Revillagigedo lost his job to the venal and incompetent brother-in-law of the Spanish chief minister. Revillagigedo was faced with trumped-up charges, but his supporters won the day and he was not imprisoned.

The British envoy, Thomas Pearce, arrived at San Blas on board a Spanish ship and went north on the *Activa* in January of 1795, meeting with Álava in Monterey. The two continued north together. On arrival, Álava ordered the fort dismantled. By the end of March, anything of value was on board the Spanish ships. The two representatives signed and countersigned the declarations. The Spanish flag was lowered and the British flag raised. The last of the Europeans went aboard the ships and sailed away to sea on March 28, 1795.

Spain's friendship with Britain was only temporary. In 1796, Spain signed a new treaty of alliance with France. A month later, Spain declared war on Britain. The Northwest Coast had been little more than a skirmish, but the rivalry between the two countries would persist well into the nineteenth century.

What was Spain's legacy on the Northwest Coast? For a brief period of time, the Northwest Coast was at the centre of European history. No usable northwest passage was found, however, denying Spain that claim to glory. In monetary terms, Spain spent much more than it gained from its presence in the Northwest. Though Spaniards sailed for both their country and for God, Spanish priests were unable to convert many of the First Nations. And yet, the Spanish names remain scattered across the map, and most of the diaries and charts were finally made public, ensuring Spain's mariners and scientists a place in the history of exploration.

Selected Bibliography

Barrington, Daines, tr. *Voyage of the Sonora from the 1775 journal of Don Francisco Antonio Mourelle*. Fairfield, WA: Ye Galleon Press, 1987.

Bodega y Quadra, Juan Francisco de la. Edition presented by Freeman Tovell, Robin Inglis and Iris H.W. Engstrand, foreword by Michael Maquinna, translated by Freeman M. Tovell. *Voyage to the Northwest Coast of America, 1792: Juan Francisco de la Bodega y Quadra and the Nootka Sound Controversy*. Norman, OK: The Arthur H. Clark Company, 2012.

Cook, Warren L. *Flood Tide of Empire: Spain and the Pacific Northwest, 1543–1819*. New Haven, CT: Yale University Press, 1973.

Cutter, Donald C., ed. *Journal of Tomás de Suría of his Voyage with Malaspina to the Northwest Coast of America*. Fairfield, WA: Ye Galleon Press, 1980.

_____ . *Malaspina & Galiano: Spanish Voyages to the Northwest Coast 1791 &1792*. Vancouver: Douglas & McIntyre, 1991.

David, Andrew, et al., ed. *The Malaspina Expedition, 1789–1794: The Journal of the Voyage by Alejandro Malaspina, Volume II*. London: Hakluyt Society; Madrid: Museo Naval, 2003.

Gough, Barry. *Juan de Fuca's Strait: Voyages in the Waterway of Forgotten Dreams*. Madeira Park: Harbour Publishing, 2012.

Kendrick, John. *The Men with Wooden Feet: The Spanish Exploration of the Pacific Northwest*. Toronto: NC Press, 1985.

McDowell, Jim. *José Narváez: the forgotten explorer: including his narrative of a voyage on the northwest coast in 1788*. Spokane, WA: Clark, 1998.

Tovell, Freeman. *At the Far Reaches of Empire: The Life of Juan Francisco de la Bodega y Quadra*. Vancouver: UBC Press, 2008.

Index